THE WEB IN THE SEA

Jung, Sophia, and the Geometry of the Soul

A Note on the Title

Life has come out of the sea, and as it did so millions of years ago, it emerged in tiny forms of exquisite design. The geometric web by which creation lifted life into being was preexistent. · ·

Its counterpart lies in the seas of our own personal and collective unconscious, as Carl Gustav Jung pointed out. Through awareness we can discover preexisting patterns that can show us meaningful order in the chaos we experience at times in the world and in our personal lives.

According to tradition, the web is woven by Sophia, Holy Wisdom, Holy Joy.

THE WEB IN THE SEA
Jung, Sophia, and the Geometry of the Soul

ALICE O. HOWELL

QUEST BOOKS
The Theosophical Publishing House

Wheaton, IL. U.S.A.
Madras, India/London, England

The Theosophical Publishing House
P.O. Box 270
Wheaton, IL 60189-0270

A publication of the Theosophical Publishing House,
a department of the Theosophical Society in America.

*This publication made possible with
the assistance of the Kern Foundation.*

Library of Congress Cataloging-in-Publication Data

Howell, Alice O., 1922-
    The web in the sea: Jung, Sophia, and the geometry of the soul/
Alice O. Howell,
        p.   cm.
    Includes bibliographical references.
    ISBN 0-8356-0688-0   (pbk.) : $14.00
    1. Spiritual life.   2. Psychology, Religious.   3. Jung, C. G.
(Carl Gustav), 1875-1961—Contributions in psychology of
religion.   4. Wisdom—Religious aspects.   5. Geometry—
Miscellanea.   6. Symbolism.   I. Title.
BF1999.H775   1993
200'.1'9—dc20
                                                    92-56482
                                                      CIP

9 8 7 6 5 4 3 2 1 ° 93 94 95 96 97 98 99

This edition is printed on acid-free paper that meets the
American National Standards Institute Z39.48 Standard

Printed in the United States of America by Versa Press

For the one whose golden ring I bear
and who bears mine—
the so dearly cherished "you" of this book,

WALTER ALFRED ANDERSEN

The Surprise

*You planted
crocuses to spell 'I love you'
one fall afternoon
while I was busy baking.
The moles were deeply touched
all winter under the snows.
Come spring
the crocuses couldn't spell at all
but I got the message from
purple, white, and yellow shouts
of glory random in the green.
We laughed
looking out the kitchen window
and talked of putting in the screens soon
for summer
but really we were thinking—
another spring,
still together.*

A.O.

Contents

	Acknowledgments	ix
I	Sophia's Secrets	1
II	Rediscovering the Wheel	19
III	Center and Circumference	31
IV	Dark within Light, Light within Dark	43
V	Filling the Cup	59
VI	Getting the Point	71
VII	Circumambulating	91
VIII	The Dividing Line	103
XI	The Power of Three	127
X	Qualities and Quantities	149
XI	Quadrillions	163
XII	Cubes within Cubes	179
XIII	The Golden Rectangle	189
XIV	Pentacles and P's and Q's	213
XV	Sixes and Sevens	225
XVI	The Web at Work	241
	Appendix: Sophia's Mondayschool	255
	Bibliography	279

Acknowledgments

I wish to thank my dear husband Walter for his tireless assistance and support during the writing of this book. Not only that, but without him, there could not have been a book. Both Christopher Bamford and Roger Woolger helped draw my attention to several valuable sources and shared them with me. Their interest and encouragement have sustained me throughout. Others helpful to me have been Mary Andersen, Rachel Fletcher, Sylvia Perera, William J. Regan, William Irwin Thompson, and Edward C. Whitmont.

I would also like to voice my appreciation for the warm hospitality over so many years of the management of the St. Columba Hotel on the Isle of Iona: Teal Picton Phillips and Angus and Alison Johnston. My thanks as well for the kindness of the Rev. Philip and Alison Newell, former Wardens of the Iona Community. My homage goes to the memory of Lord Fuinary, George MacLeod, whose efforts restored the Abbey of Iona, and who founded the Iona Community, and whose cheery letters to me were so deeply appreciated.

In conclusion, I wish to thank Shirley Nicholson again for her able guidance as editor and friend, as well as Brenda Rosen, her most helpful successor.

The creation of shapes through the use of numbers and geometry, as mathematical expressions, recalls the Archetypes reflected through the World of Symbols. Mathematics then, is a language of the intellect, a means of spiritual hermeneutics whereby one can move from the sensible to the intelligible world.

—Laleh Bakhtiar

This magical art, sometimes called 'the knowledge and conversation of the holy guardian angel,' attempts to bring about a conscious relationship with the interior guiding spirit, whether this is conceived of as the conscience, the angel or the daemon. This is one of the most important functions of Sophia in that she is the angelic presence whom all may seek. Because she is established in these texts [Wisdom and Ecclesiasticus] as the partner both of God and of the soul, she is likewise the symbol of divine union—the sacred marriage of heaven to earth.

—Caitlin Matthews

[To the Pythagoreans] the contemplation of the divine Law, which was the content of the study of mathematics, was a direct contact with a divine Reality: Divinity immanent in the cosmos.

—Cornelia de Vogel

When we see God, we see him not by reason, but by something that is higher than reason. It is impossible, however, to say about him who sees that he sees, because he does not behold and discern two different things (the seer and the thing seen). He changes completely, ceases to be himself, preserves nothing of his "I." Immersed in God, he constitutes one whole with Him; like the center of a circle, which coincides with the center of a greater circle.

—Plotinus (205?-270 A.D.)

Nothing stands between me and God but the word "I."
—Yunus Emre (14th century Turkish Sufi poet)

I

Sophia's Secrets

The name *Hagia Sophia*, Holy Wisdom, Holy Spirit, is becoming more familiar to people everywhere. According to various prophecies Sophia has a special connection to the Isle of Iona. In the Old Testament, Wisdom is called cocreator of the world, which implies that she is a feminine principle or "goddess." Such a term may shock some Christian sensibilities—it would have mine in the past—and so it is essential for me to define "gods and goddesses of old" as *personifications* of universal processes or archetypes. Since they are universal, humanity has considered them to be "divine." They were symbolic and descriptive extensions of that great mystery we name God. To look at gods and goddesses this way opens us to greater compassion, tolerance, and understanding of humanity past and present. To understand this specific definition at the outset is most important.

When I was a child, my mother explained to me that she could be a daughter, a wife, a mother, a neighbor, an author, and on and on, and yet essentially remain herself. The various terms given were based on her relationships. We used to play a game extending ourselves to dog-owners, bread-eaters, tax-payers, and on and on. I learned in this way to see how one person could by extension become many, and later on it helped me to grasp the multiple names and extensions given to the mysterious One God, Light of Lights, that we struggle to grasp and to name and cannot. I learned early on in this fashion that we need not limit or reject the different ways we and others may relate to the sacred.

Here in the West we tend to fall too easily into literalizing and concretizing. So to call wisdom by the name "Sophia" might imply to some that this separates her from the same archetype that goes by other names in other cultures. Naming and personifying wisdom, in this instance, gives her life in human experience. We ourselves are personifications of our essence. We came from somewhere and return somewhere, leaving that personification behind; yet we can hope to continue. A so-called god or a goddess, being archetypal, is for keeps. The names may change, the idols built in their honor may be smashed, but the essential nature of what they personify remains. One cannot kill an archetype. Archetypes are living principles of a kind that move the world, but they come closer to our understanding if we can relate to them in a personal way by naming them. And yet we can remain in awe of their mystery when we perceive them in a transpersonal way.

At the very outset, it is vital to understand what Hagia Sophia represents here: the loving, intimate, kind, helpful, and practical aspect of Holy Wisdom in each individual and, at the same time, the great ordering principle of the physical creation of the cosmos. The function of her archetype is to unite both of these principles through greater consciousness and love. She is the *anima mundi*, the soul of the world, for some, or the *lumen naturae*, the light within nature, for others. At the simplest level, for the child in us, she may even disguise herself as the Fairy Godmother or the beloved guardian angel. To Socrates, her name was the daemon. Jesus called her the Paraclete, the Comforter. Early Christians called her Hagia Sophia, the Holy Spirit or Holy Ghost. Her symbol then and now is the dove.

Hagia and *Sophia* are Greek words. They were translated into Latin as *Spiritus Sanctus*, a masculine proper noun, requiring a masculine pronoun. So Wisdom's essential feminine nature in both the Hebrew of the Old Testament and the Greek of the New Testament got lost in the Latin translation. This eventually turned the Christian Trinity or triangle of the Godhead into a totally masculine one, leaving out the feminine, women, and Mother Nature completely. Mat[t]er became an "it" to conquer, rape, and manipulate through power.

I am not a theologian, but perhaps somebody could bring this to the attention of some. Oddly enough, a friend sent me word of one, a Professor Jurgen Moltman, who wrote the following in the *Scottish Journal of Theology*, citing the work of Macarius the Egyptian/Symeon:

> Hebrew and Syriac are languages which themselves make it easy to call the Holy Spirit "the heavenly Mother" for both *ruach* and *ruho* are feminine words. But Macarius has two essential theological arguments for the motherly function of the Holy Spirit: 1. He

links John 14:26 with Isaiah 66:13—the Holy Spirit is the Paraclete, the promised Comforter. . . . 2. Only the person "who is born anew" can see the kingdom of God. And people are born anew from the Spirit (John 3:3-5). So believers are "children of the Spirit." The Spirit is their "Mother." . . . The motherly image makes it possible to grasp the *personal* character of the Holy Spirit more precisely than other images. The motherly image makes it more possible to understand the unique *community* of the Trinity better than other concepts of the Spirit. Incidentally, the dove as symbol for the Holy Spirit is also a feminine image and points in the same direction. "The fellowship of the Holy Spirit" in its feminine and motherly character operates sympathetically on men and women, healing them and liberating them.

Now that's my idea of a theologian!

As archetypal Comforter, Sophia speaks to us—if we will listen—within our souls and wakens us to remembering who we really are. Her motto is *"Ego coniungo,"* I unite.

After writing about Sophia in *The Dove in the Stone: Finding the Sacred in the Commonplace*, I returned to Iona several times with my dear husband Walter to reflect upon yet another aspect of Sophia's wisdom. This book is the result. The topic we discussed was sacred geometry as we experience it within ourselves. This book is intended to serve as a humble introduction and primer at the very simplest of levels. It is my hope that Sophia's function of mediating between our outer and inner worlds and between what Jung termed our ego and our Self will prove to be a source of insight and delight. My greatest hope is to stimulate others to further exploration of the subject. The study of sacred geometry for me has been like walking as a small child in the huge footsteps tracked across the ages by some great and profound lovers of Sophia, which is what *philo-sopher* means.

Sophia lies hidden all about us in the testament of form and design. Alas, we take the obvious for granted so easily and think it to be the last place to look for wisdom. Yet this is one of her games. If you play her hide-and-seek, you will discover that Ring-around-a-rosy and the ring of eternity have something in common—circular motion. The cowlick on a baby's head and the spiral of a galaxy follow the same mathematical laws. For me, it is a lot less scary and intimidating to start looking for symbolic wisdom in kindergarten and move on up to Pythagoras, Plato and Proclus. In that sense I have never left elementary school, and as I grow older, I appreciate more and more why Jung sculpted the child Telesphorus at the center of the Bollingen Stone and why Jesus said that we would have to become like little children to enter the kingdom of heaven.

In the last several centuries the symbolic nature— the very soul, if you will—has been removed from most of the sciences. Alchemy was rejected by chemistry; astrology by astronomy; and the inner meaning of numbers and geometric structures, found everywhere in nature and creation, was removed from mathematics as having any sacred meaning. All the aforementioned sciences are, by and large, applied to practical, "scientific" technology today, and their spiritual connections or implications have been tossed aside as quaint and archaic superstitions. The result is the present ecological peril of the planet and of all life forms dwelling upon it. Science, more than anything in this world, needs to reconnect to the spiritual implications of its own discoveries. For this we need to use the gift within our souls, something far more precious than intellect alone— the gift of feminine wisdom. Logos has lost his bride, Sophia.

In old Anglo-Saxon, the word *wisdom* is very clear: it is *inwit*. *Inwit* is Sophia dwelling within us. Besides being wise, she is oftentimes witty, dancing circles around the hoary-bearded theologians and phi- losophers and giggling sympathetically at their efforts, as well as at the solemnity of my good in- tentions and, perhaps, yours. My childhood Fairy Godmother was called Mercy Muchmore. I can hear her saying to me, "Did you ever meet a bluebell trying to be good? Or a theological duck?" Being human sometimes seems to mean thinking too *much*. It can get in the way of reality. To be present in the moment is to be gratefully aware. How is that different? I would ask. "That's mind plus—," she would say. Plus what? That is one of Sophia's secrets and what this book is about.

In ancient China, India, Egypt, Greece, and North Africa, and in primitive and native cultures of the New World, the connection between numbers and shapes and nature was understood and revered. Ancient peoples practiced a "theology of numbers." In fact, in ancient Sumeria there were two number systems, one sacred and one profane. The sacred was based on multiples of 6 and derived from astronomical calculations. We have inherited this in our calculation of time: 60 seconds to a minute; 60 minutes to an hour; 24 hours to a day; 360 degrees to a circle; in our measurements of 12 inches to a foot and 3 feet to a yard; in the ubiquity of the number 12 in the zodiac; in your eggbox; in a jury—and there are many others. By contrast, they used the decimal system for business, since the human body provides us with a dactylic abacus in our fingers and toes. Beyond the number 20, a score, you could use pebbles. Our word "calculate" comes from the Latin word *calculus*, meaning *pebble*.

In my childhood in English schools we had to struggle with both systems because 12 pennies made a shilling, but 20 shillings made a pound, and for extra special you had 21 shillings to a guinea. Certainly the decimal system is more practical, but perhaps there lingers an unconscious reluctance to give up all of our sacred numbering.

In ancient times each number had a shape and a character of its own. Once you had an inkling of this, the ancients believed, you had a key to reading the outer world symbolically for its inner, spiritual meaning. There was also an understanding that mathematical harmonies in music, numbers, and shapes were the fundament of all creation. "God geometrizes," they said.

I was curious to know *why* a circle was a symbol for God and a square a symbol for matter. We can discover the answers through personal experience. (This is well worth the bother, as it is one of Sophia's keys to wisdom.) I found that these assignations were not just arbitrary items to learn through parroting formulae but genuine revelations. Numbers and geometric shapes are just so. They come with the territory and are built into our cosmos, and they are irrefutable. This is why they were said to reside in the realm of the ideal. We can argue about the meaning of words till the cows come home, but a square is a square is a square. Today we know that we see circles and squares and numbers with our right brain, so we see them holistically rather than linearly. We experience them, rather than think them.

I try to remind myself of this as I labor over adding the sales tax to my purchases or balancing my checkbook or even making change with magical little circles of copper and nickel. (They, too have profound meaning! The shape of value is round, whole.)

For many mathematicians of old, this irrefutable order was nothing less than a "proof" of whatever we mean by God. The relationship between chaos and order is a dance of love. Chaos is at the end of any toy kaleidoscope, and order at the other end. Chaos is my vision of the inside of any multicolored sweater I have knitted, and order is the miracle of the other side. Chaos was a Greek god. I know him well. He lives in my office on weekends. But to the Greeks, he was the father of Gaia, our earth. Chaos as a cosmic process or a mental one is a cause for terror. Yet, even the great physical catastrophes that beset nature are healed in good time. Flowers grow out of ashes, trees spring up from flooded land, and the dead and the detritus, if natural, are recycled year after year. It is only what we as human beings are doing that is unnatural, that is damaging the earth, and we are doing these dreadful things because we cannot see that the earth itself is a living whole and a conscious one, as Teilhard de Chardin has suggested. We have forgotten this, but the native people of the world still understand and could teach us much about it.

In the "good old days," intellect was used to discover meaning. The ego, center of consciousness according to Jung, served the philosophers of the time to find out how they might become wiser, not richer or more powerful. So the revelation that numbers and shapes pre-existed humankind must have been deeply affecting. It was tantamount to discovering the deepest source of security and measure. The solar system runs on time, even if we don't. Harmony and proportion, the very underpinnings of beauty in nature, art, and relationship, were discovered, uncovered, and made conscious by humankind. And we know today that we could not recognize beauty if we did not have it within us. The examples that we have in classical Greece and Egypt alone take the breath away. The geometry of those periods and its sacred implications resurfaced much later in the Gothic cathedrals of the Middle Ages and the stunning architecture of the Renaissance.

It was not until the Renaissance that art and religion in Europe lost their strict moral connection. In the new climate of humanism, art was freed to be free and has enriched the world in new ways ever since, but geometry eventually became a tool for design rather than for symbolic insights. Sacred geometry, so rich and dear to the ancients, became inimical to the power of the Church. Perhaps it was perceived as too pagan, too arcane or kabbalistic. Thus it was forced to go underground where it was kept alive in certain guilds and secret fraternities. It hid in alchemical symbols and drawings, in Freemasonry, in Rosicrucian brotherhoods, in both Tarot and playing cards. Though much of it has continued to survive in Christian symbolism, it very rarely is taught as something to attend to. Only in the last fifty years are new revelations coming to the surface and becoming readily available to the inquiring mind. Learning about sacred geometry is like learning a new language, a new way of seeing and perceiving the wealth of wisdom and meaning hidden in both natural and constructed form. Its silent teaching comes to us through the pupil of the eye. It is a constant in nature but is capable of bursting out around us in sudden happenstances and serendipities. It requires not only looking but noticing.

Take a break from reading this and look around wherever you happen to be. Observe how many geometrical shapes are around you. If you are indoors there are rectangular windows and doors, books. There are surely squares in tiles, lines curving in pictures, furniture, wallpaper; surfaces and planes; circular plates and coins viewed with your own circular eyes. If there is a child about, set her or him to counting and discovering how many shapes there are.

Should you be outside in nature, the abundance of evidence is even greater, for not a flower nor a snowflake, not a tree nor a bush can grow without following geometric laws of progression. If you stop to fully realize it, any flower knowing how to push itself sunwards out of brown earth and burst into fragrant diadems is a miracle that could keep the most jaded among us going and trusting in the wonder of the process of growth.

It is that same inner thrust within the psyche, according to Jung, that pushes us up into being who we really are supposed to be. This is the profound secret of individuation: as all growing things in outer nature yearn sunwards, so do we yearn for that inward sun and light within us that sheds meaning to our own existence. One of Sophia's greatest secrets is that nature's processes are true of the psyche as well *but reversed*. Another example of this is that it takes a father and a mother to produce a child. Within the psyche, the inversion is equally true as process. It takes a "divine" father and a "virgin" mother within us to consummate a *hierosgamos* or sacred marriage to bring us to a "second birth," a spiritual rebirth. This is the underlying archetypal and symbolic pattern of the parentage of spiritual saviors the world over: Buddha, Krishna, Lao Tzu, and Jesus Christ among them. These great examples in history are paradigms for what all humanity is said eventually to be capable of. In themselves, they came to teach us how to accomplish this. All the great teachers hint in one way or another of this symbolic inversion, that the outer but mirrors the inner reality. The philosophers had a code for this secret: they simple took the symbol of Mercury [☿] which stood for thinking and turned it upside down [☿].

The funny thing is that our bodies verify this. Our eyes see things upside down and crossways, and the brain reverses the incoming images. We live, as one scientist calls it, in a "reflexive universe." Look in any mirror and it teaches reversal. Psychologically speaking, the outer world we see is truly a "looking glass of circumstance" ever there to teach us. (I found this phrase in a letter written by an eight-year-old boy to Bronson Alcott in 1836.) This secret of Sophia is both simple and profound.

Getting back to sacred geometry among the ancients, it flourished in India, and still does, and also in the world of Islam. Those in the esoteric branches of Hinduism, Buddhism, and Islam (Sufis) probably know more about the subject than any other people. But now we are finding out that the Celts and pre-Celts also had a sophisticated if not positively grandiose vision of the subject. Such phenomena as the circles of standing stones and the Glastonbury Zodiac (thirty miles in circumference) and the ley lines are yielding more and more proof that here, too, geometry was used for sacred reasons, based on astronomical reckoning that boggles the mind.

We cannot know how it affected these ancient people inwardly, but it is evident that the goddess was also worshiped in Britain and Ireland. The standing stones of Callanish on the Isle of Lewis in the Outer Hebrides are oriented to the moon, and another circle of stones there is oriented to a long reclining figure of a woman visible in a range of undulating hills, still called *An cailleach*, the woman. Every Saros cycle, or 223 lunations (18 years and 11 1/3 days), the moon rises either from her lap or her head.

According to the Indian scholar Sir John Woodruffe, the root of the words *man, mind,* and *month* all go back to the same Sanskrit root *man*, one meaning of which is "moon." Perhaps this was a prehistoric source of measuring. Maat (Egypt), Me (Babylon), and Metis (Greek) all were goddesses of both wisdom and order. It is but a step to *mater* (mother) and *meter* and *matter*. So for millennia the collective unconscious has associated the highest aspect of the feminine with wisdom and order.

By *feminine*, I do not mean gender only but the basic universal process of both being receptive and being capable of giving new form to life. This capacity is generally internalized in both men and women, and externalized in reproduction by mothers. The words *economics* and *ecology* that we hear so much today also have feminine connotations, since their root *eco* means "home" in Greek. The earth is truly our home, and Sophia's presence is needed to bring it back to a place of wisdom and beauty and order. The "seven pillars of wisdom" belong to Sophia, and three of these are arithmetic, geometry, and astronomy. So Sophia has always been recognized as the personification of the skillful formation of creation. Only mothers can give form to life in giving birth to children. So at the transpersonal level, Sophia is both mother of nature (Mother Nature) and mother of the God within us (Godmother).

One of Sophia's most important functions, psychologically speaking, is to "make sense" out of the chaos of our personal and collective lives. You can call upon her when you balance your checkbook, and Lord knows, we need her to balance the national budget! More important, we can call upon her to reveal the meaning behind our suffering and confusion. She is, according to the Old Testament, "the Comforter, kind and friendly, to humankind." Sophia is the personification of wisdom, and Hagia Sophia, we must remember, is Holy Wisdom.

Today, many skeptics laugh at the idea of "good

or bad vibrations," but the fact remains that, in terms
of physics, everything has its own rate of vibration,
be it sound or color or light, and these occur in
successive octaves. It is also significant that as
human beings, we are subject to a kind of threshold
which limits the ability of our senses to respond
to certain higher or lower pitches of sound or spectra
of color. Now we know this. We also know that this
limitation implies that there is a great deal we do
not know, and normally cannot know. Yet some
people can function at other levels of knowing, and
they do. Sophia can teach us that we, too, by experiencing things at a limited level of vibration,
can intuit much that takes place on other levels,
because the "laws" or the "processes" are consistent.
"As above, so below" implies that "so below" could
teach us quite a bit about "as above."

Knowing that there is an "above" puts an entirely
different complexion on nature, as such, and the way
that we look at it. It also implies that with the help
of Sophia, we can learn a great deal more about
ourselves and the wonder that we are through
learning how to read, see, hear, and experience the
symbolic language that is *already* expressed by spirit
in earth. "The kingdom of heaven is spread upon
the earth but men do not see it," Jesus says in *The
Gospel according to Thomas*. "Cleave the wood and I
am there, break the stone and I am there."

Carl Gustav Jung, the great Swiss psychologist,
was a pioneer in approaching the mystical aspects
of sciences like astronomy and chemistry from a
psychological point of view, for which he was at

first ridiculed by his peers. But as the years pass, his efforts to look at these matters objectively are beginning to make sense. In the end, much of Jung's work has helped restore the spiritual implications of the sciences.

At first Jung's approach to these rejected aspects (such as alchemy and astrology) was to say that if they were the product of the human psyche, then they are worthy of study from the psychological standpoint. He led the way, with scrupulous scholarship, to approaching this complex material in a new and creative fashion. He began to see the psychological value of these so-called alchemical processes, and he understood that the object of the research of the alchemists was not just turning the metal lead into gold, but the transmutation of painful experience in this world (Saturn=lead) to spiritual gold, the gold of individuation and enlightenment. *Non aurum vulgum*, not vulgar gold, they wrote.

By the same token, Jung restored a new dignity to astrology, seeing its psychological value. The chart for him was a description of how a person might be likely to process experience. It was Jung, as well, who connected the Sanksrit word *mandala* (circle) specifically to the idea of the Self as the center and totality of the psyche—the microcosm of the individual living in the macrocosm of the universe. Thus Jung reconnected geometry for us in the West with its spiritual aspect. He was fully aware that Hindu yogis had never lost the connection, and, indeed, carried it to great heights in the richness of symbolism in *tantra* (the chakra system), *yantra* (geometric diagrams for meditation), and *mantra* (sacred syllables that affect consciousness). That sound forms geometric shapes is now a demonstrable fact, and this is the object of the study known as cymatics.

Today there are fortunately a good number of people writing the most wonderful books on the subject of sacred geometry. You will find a reading list in the appendix. I, myself, flounder in the higher mathematics of the subject, and so I am restricting myself—very humbly, indeed—to sharing my own personal wonder and delight in this aspect of Sophia.

So my approach here is like that of a child listening to a Fairy Godmother, such as my own Mercy Muchmore. If I am irreverent, please forgive me! Those who know, know. But to quote T. H. White, "We can't all and most of us don't!" The majority of people that I encounter have never even heard of this subject, and yet when they do, they become as excited as I am. We need only to remember that we are beginning to understand that we live in a holistic world, and so what we observe today in the outer world has its parallel in our inner world. As observers, as men and women living upon this earth, we are subsumed as creatures. We ourselves are created beings, with the power to cocreate. It is in this creative *process* that we are "made in the image of God." It is the Sophia in us that is the Paraclete, the "Comforter" and guide. So, with that in mind, back to Iona we go!

God is a circle whose center is everywhere and whose circumference is nowhere.
                                    —Nicholas of Cusa (among others)

There is one mind common to all individual men. Every man is an inlet into all of the same. He that is once admitted to the right of reason is made a freeman of the whole estate. What Plato has thought, he may think; what a saint has felt, he may feel; what at any time has befallen any man, he can understand. Who hath access to this universal mind is a party to all that is or can be done, for this is the only and sovereign agent.
                                    —Ralph Waldo Emerson

We sit around in a circle and suppose
And the secret sits in the middle and knows.
                                    —Robert Frost

. . . God is a universal Self, while the individual self is the "heaven within us" something supra-sensible and divine . . .
                                    —Carl Gustav Jung
                                    quoting the Japanese sage Ikea

I usually describe the supraordinate personality as the 'self,' thus making a sharp distinction between the ego, which, as is well known, extends only as far as the conscious mind, and the whole of the personality, which includes the unconscious as well as the conscious component. The ego is thus related to the self as part to whole. To that extent the self is supraordinate. Moreover, the Self is felt empirically not as subject but as object, and this by reason of its unconscious component, which can only come to consciousness indirectly, by way of projection. Because of its unconscious component the self is so far removed from the conscious mind that it can only be partially expressed by human figures; the other part of it has to be expressed by objective abstract symbols . . . [the] geometrical figures like the circle, the sphere, the square, the quaternity, the clock, the firmament and so on.
                                    —Carl Gustav Jung

II
Rediscovering the Wheel

It was a fresh September morning. Glorious. We had safely returned to Iona. After a good Scottish breakfast of porridge and kippers, we decided to head north to *Traigh ban nam Manach*, the White Strand of the Monks. We were going to make a day of it, so we carried a picnic lunch and a thermos of tea. Briskly, we set off up the narrow road, the blue waters of the Sound of Iona to our right and the great pyramid of Dun I, Iona's only mountain, to our left. We passed the abbey and then a succession of fields, some dotted with golden haycocks, others with grazing sheep. A tractor grumbled by with a farmer and his collie sitting together in the driver's cab. We waved. Since it was a Wednesday, there were no pilgrims. Soon we were virtually on our own. Unabashed, white heads and all, we held hands, matching our paces, feeling far younger than we were. We had little need to talk. Each was savoring the happiness of the other.

"What are you thinking?" you asked me, when we stopped to rest on a bench along the way.

"I'm thinking of Snuffy MacDuff and how much

he would enjoy this," I said. Snuffy is our feisty brindle cairn back home. I pictured him bouncing ahead in bursts of "hoppiness," as you call it, with his raggedy ears pointed up and his tail held merrily, ready to bark at anything new. "I think Snuffy really is a great teacher. He lives so completely in the present," I mused.

You had to agree, and I wondered if I am able to live in the now. On Iona I always have the sense of living in some other kind of time and space. It is as if one savors every moment with the idea that it can be relived. I am reliving it this very minute as I write. I can truly feel my footsteps and the slight bluffing of the breeze in my ears. I can smell the tide and the hay, hear the baa-ing of the sheep, relish the dear warmth of your hand holding mine to the left, with the sturdy bole of Woodstock, my Scottish cromag or walking stick, on the right. Is this past or present, I wonder. I close my eyes and do not quite know.

"What were you thinking?" I asked in turn.

"I was thinking how much we owe to Carl Gustav Jung. If it hadn't been for him, we would never have met, and we never would be walking together to this beach." This was true. We had met on a ship between Venice and Greece on which I was lecturing, along with others, on Jung and the archetypal features of the ancient religions of Mediterranean cultures. It had been the trip of a lifetime: Egypt, Israel, Turkey, Patmos, Greece, Yugoslavia, and Italy. It had exposed us not only to ancient religions, but to Islam, Judaism, and Christianity, in both its Eastern Orthodoxy and Western Catholicism, and various other sects, as well. We, a sizable group of pilgrims from the New World, were committed to visiting the power points and holy sites of the old one. It was quite a profound experience on many levels. It led to our happy marriage, now ten years old.

Presently we went through a large swinging cattle gate that crossed the road. After carefully closing it behind us, we made our way down the grassy dunes to the shelter of the beach, continuing our conversation.

I ventured that Jung's contributions to depth psychology might eventually hold a solution for the lack of understanding among the great religions. I told you again that I felt that Jung would someday be recognized, not just as a great psychiatrist, but as a real spiritual prophet of the coming age, because the concepts and the language that he developed provide a basis for mutual understanding. In fact, it could be demonstrated geometrically. Slowly and carefully I did my best to explain this succinctly, never an easy task.

Jung proposed that there is such a thing as the collective unconscious or objective psyche through which all humanity and, perhaps, all of creation shares a common pool or substratum of wisdom and experience. Each life contributes its experience to it, and each individual has the potential capacity to tap into it. It lies beyond or beneath the personal unconscious, that part of the individual psyche that contains the suppressed and repressed personal memories of our present life. Just as the individual psyche contains archetypal contents with different functions—anima, animus, ego, shadow, etc.—so does the collective on a mythological scale.

The great gods and goddesses of old, part of the

collective unconscious, were personifications of universal processes, considered from the beginning as divine. Through the centuries, they have been named and renamed in different cultures and destroyed in iconoclastic frenzy by conflicting fanatics. Yet the archetypes themselves remain indestructible, because they are as fundamental to creation as energy is in its different expressions. We cannot destroy existence—sunlight, darkness, weather, or the sexes, for instance—but we can easily smash or ridicule the concepts or idols of others representing them. We do this in our folly and righteous ignorance, not understanding that you cannot kill an archetype! It will only reappear carrying the new name and appearance of our human projection. We will identify with them and swear that they are the real thing, and they are—in the sense that what they *represent* is absolutely real. What we need to remember is that the concretizations are ephemeral. As Goethe wrote: *Alles Vergängliche ist nur ein Gleichnis* (All things transitory are only a likeness). If we could only see through matter to its metaphor, we could read and reread all things symbolically until we stood in the presence of the truth, that truth that can only be experienced, never described.

Century after century, millennium after millennium, the pattern is repeated. New names for eternal archetypes emerge, rise, and fall in the name of a "religion." We cannot be against religion, but to be for it, we need to see the deeper purpose common to all religions. And by that, I tried to explain, I mean Jung's profound psychological purpose in appealing to the divinity within each individual.

Only a few weeks ago, I cut out a political cartoon. It depicted six uniformed and armed soldiers on their knees with hands uplifted in prayer. Each had a label on his back: "Jew," "Arab," "Hindu," "Muslim," "Protestant," and "Catholic." The prayer of the Jew was "Kill the Arabs!"; the prayer of the Arab was "Kill the Jews!"; the prayers of the Hindu and Muslim were mutually the same, and each of the two Christians prayed for the other's destruction.

Don't you think, I said, warming to the subject, that as one humanity, we are one species? We share a common pattern of skeleton and structure. We share a common normal temperature. We share common physical features. More important but not yet understood, *we share a common pattern of psyche*. Jung, through his studies of over 64,000 dreams, demonstrated their archetypal contents to be similar. Dreams of fair or destructive women, heroic or cowardly men, villains, monsters, nature, children, caves, and oceans; scenes of challenge, danger, sexual encounters, fires, drownings, joyous events— all are common to people living anywhere in the world. From Berlin to Brooklyn to Bombay to the Bahamas, we dream the same kinds of dreams.

Jung also felt that buried in every psyche is the religious instinct, the quest for God, for meaning, and for self-realization. For many this instinct has been satisfied through projecting it outward in shared symbols and sacred rituals. This has been a collective experience, but because of evolution and education, many people are now withdrawing the security offered by these projections. These people constitute the growing number of men and women who have for one reason or another rejected

religion and find themselves at a loss to find a
meaning to life within themselves or a sense of inner
worth. It is the dilemma of a modern humanity
which has lost its soul. In despair, we live shallow
lives or turn to drink, sex, drugs, or anything that
will help us flee "the hound of heaven."

As the panorama of history has unfolded, great
teachers have come into this world, all bearing a
message: This is the Only Way. Gautama Buddha,
Krishna, Moses, Jesus, Mohammed, Ramakrishna, and
many, many of the hidden teachers have all said this
same thing. And we, being foolish, miss the point.
We say to ourselves, if one of them is right, then
the others must be wrong. Great new religious cultures and customs, rituals and symbols, cluster
around each of the Teachers, once they have
departed, and fights and wars and misunderstandings
break out and never cease. What we have failed to
realize—and what Jung makes it possible for us to
grasp—is that all of these teachers were individuated
beings who were describing the same "way" from
personal experience—namely the Only Way or
process (verb!) by which the human psyche can
become spiritually fulfilled. This Way is a "how"
not a "what," and that is the secret. It is an unfolding
drama within the individual soul.

If you study the mystical or *esoteric* traditions
of each of the great religions, you will find similarities
rather than differences. Most of us have to be satisfied
with believing, but some know. The real Teachers
seem to come again and again to tell us that we, too,
can know.

You laughed at my intensity and playfully ruffled
my hair. "Come down to the water," you laughed.

"Let me show you something, and then you tell me what you think. You gave me an idea."

We walked down to where the beach was smooth, hard, and firm. You borrowed Woodstock and drew a diagram in the sand. It looked like this:

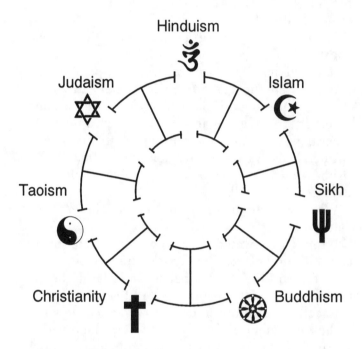

"If what you are saying is true, then it is as if all the great exoteric religions offer an entrance to a central mystery, the dot in the middle. So, supposing you as a Hindu and I as a Christian go into our respective temples and follow the teachings of our respective scriptures to the best of our ability. Then it might be possible for both of us, through understanding the *symbolic* import of what we are doing, to discover an *inner* process—by inner, I mean inside of us as individuals—that would lead us further into the inner circle."

I was dumbfounded.

"You see," you continued, "once you get to the inner circle there are no more divisions."

I nodded my head.

"I don't know where to put the atheists and agnostics—"

I chimed in, "Atheists are probably people who have rejected the god of the level beneath them. Agnostics are like those who would run around the circle never going in one of the entrances or, at least, just sticking their noses in the door and sniffing. I always remember something that Rama-krishna said: 'Digging a lot of shallow holes will never get you a well.' "

"What would you call the inner circle?" you wondered.

"I think that would be the esoteric tradition of each of the religions. The mystical tradition."

"You mean like the Kabbalah for Judaism, or the Sufi tradition in Islam—that kind of teaching?"

"Exactly. The esoteric or inner practice depends on the enactment of the outer mystery deep within the soul of the individual. Each religion provides for this. So when the individual reaches that inner light, he or she cannot fail to recognize it in others. All religions consider such people as saints, and they are depicted with a halo or a nimbus around them. The Sufis show a man whose head is a flame of light, of love. The Buddha has a raised peak to his head. And the enlightened ones of Africa and South America are also shown as having something emerging from the top of their heads. It shows the connection to higher consciousness."

"And Christianity?"

"Christianity is full of mystical traditions and teaching. It always has been. But there have been times when such teachings were seen as potentially giving too much power to individuals outside of the hierarchy. Mystics were often persecuted and put to death. We were consigned to the exoteric, the outer teaching. It got pretty bad, historically speaking, as you know."

"What about the Reformation?" you asked.

I recounted how Jung maintained that Luther led straight to Freud and the discovery of the personal unconscious, because the outer symbolic trappings, beautiful as they were, were removed from the Protestant Church, forcing each person to confront the mystery within the psyche. This is a scary thing, at first, especially as this was a new experiment in the Western world, and there were few to show the Way to do it.

I went on to say that in the last hundred years, other attempts at revealing how to go about it have emerged—such as Theosophy and Anthroposophy. The ideas they present were ridiculed by some at first, but as science has made more strides, people should take another look. Truth, such as it is, can only be hinted at. The rest, alas, is up to us as individuals. We can only understand what we are ready to understand.

You stood still on the beach, your white head bent over, your attention elsewhere. You were frowning and fussing over your parka, snapping and unsnapping one of the snaps. I thought you might be cold.

"What's the matter?" I asked.

Then you looked up with a rakish grin. "It's another Aha! It's perfect. Just look." I bent over to study the snap. "See," you demonstrated, "they're circles. One is a he and one is a she. You snap them together and they make One out of Two, like me and you. And that's sheer poetry," you added gleefully. Whereupon you threw your arms around me with a happy shout. "Sophia is great! Let's eat!"

I laughed all the way through lunch. Now I would never see a snap the same way ever again—"Holy Snaps!"

. . . it's strange how many people only picture God as transcendent, making himself known by shooting off thunderbolts. God is transcendent, above the world and beyond it, outside time and space in a mode of being which is beyond the scope of our imaginations to conceive, but the God who makes Himself known to us is the immanent God, the God who's so close that he's at the very center of our existence. It's strange too how much time people spend travelling round and round the circle of existence and getting nowhere. The real journey—the journey all people are required to take to achieve integration, self-realisation, and fulfillment—"the eternal life" of religious language—is the journey inwards, the journey to the centre of the soul.

— Susan Howatch, 1992

I set out from the wide ground of Spirit. This is; all else is its manifestation. Body is Spirit at its circumference. It denotes its confines to the external sense; it individualizes, defines Spirit, breaks the Unity into Multiplicity and places under the vision of man parts of the great Whole which, standing thus separate, can be taken in by the mind—too feeble to apprehend the Whole at a single view. —Infinitude is too wide for man to take in. He is therefore permitted to take in portions and spread his vision over the wide circumference by little and little; and in these portions doth the Infinite shadow forth itself, God in all and all in God.

—Bronson Alcott's Journal, 1835

Spirituality is not to be learned by flight from the world, by running away from things, or by turning solitary and going apart from the world. Rather we must learn to penetrate things and find God here.

—Meister Eckhart

Virtutes divinae in res diffusae.
(Qualities divine are diffused in things.)

—Cornelius Agrippa von Nettesheim

III

Center and Circumference

We lay back against the warm sands of the dunes and gazed out at the sparkling waters of the sea. They had become bright blue, and the tide having turned, the waters were sliding inexorably closer up the beach. I sifted sand softly through my fingers, remembering that my son had once told me why sand remains separate particles and does not turn to dust. It seems each separate grain attracts its own protective womb of water which buffers it from the other grains.

No one else was about, and had it not been for a bright red buoy bobbing up and down in the distance, the view might well have not changed much since St. Columba's day. I was feeling lazy but I decided to walk down to wade in cold water. We both took off our shoes and socks and picked our way through the strands of dried seaweed and sharp shells down to the flat wet sand at the water's edge. We inhaled the fresh saltiness of the air.

"Well, how does Jung explain the only Way?" you asked, picking up our former conversation.

Now it was my turn to draw a circle in the sand.

I used the edge of a shell and so it was by no means as perfect a circle as on this page, but a circle it was. Next I put a dot in the middle of it.

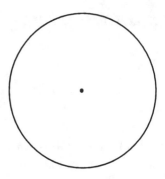

"This is the best way I can explain it." I then related how Jung defined the Self as the center and totality of the human psyche. He compared this Self at times to the Sun of our inner solar system, quoting Origen and Paracelsus. At other times he compared it to the Hindu concept of the Atman or to the Christian term "the Christ Within." The Sufis call it "the Beloved." I, myself, sometimes refer to it as "the Divine Guest." So despite any religious affiliation, anyone can accept this Self as a psychological fact. The word *Self* has to be clearly distinguished from the concept of *selfishness*, which in English means egotism. Jung maintained that this central Self lives in the unconscious in another dimension, beyond time or space.

I like that idea, because it takes away the fear of death. Part of each of us is already in that dimension all the time, though we are not usually aware of it at the level of the ego. We just rejoin it at death.

This is a wonderfully comforting thought to anyone growing older. I think that's why the Teachers say, "Die before you die." Then you discover for certain that this Self dwells in you, for a fact. It is only the ego that gets scared of dying.

We stood contemplating the circle. Several gulls swooped down to join in the study. They gleamed white and grey. I never saw such clean looking gulls.

"Where's the ego?" you asked.

"Whizzing around just inside the circumference, mediating between the outer world of environment and experience and the inner world of meaning. We even use the expression 'running around in circles,' don't we! The ego keeps searching, and oddly enough that word comes from the Latin word *circare*, which means to go around in circles."

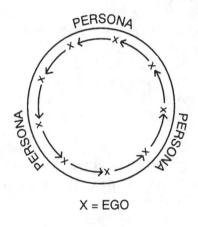

X = EGO

"What would the actual circumference represent then?"

"Perhaps what Jung termed the persona, the outer

mask that we wear in the world to protect ourselves and others."

"What's my persona like?" you asked.

"Oh, you have a sensible, confident businessman persona. Very dignified and conventional. No one would ever guess how wonderfully silly you can be."

You grinned. "That's probably true. You are ruining my persona. Oh, dear."

"Not really. We have access to several, I'm sure, just like we have different clothes for different occasions. It would be devastating to get stuck identified with one persona. Imagine being a solemn undertaker twenty-four hours a day or a 'good ole boy' or a snobbish intellectual. It would turn your circumference into an eggshell, and you couldn't hatch."

"I think I see what you mean," you said dubiously. "It's better not to get stuck in only one role. Say some more about the ego. The word means *I*, so it must mean who I think I am—me."

I explained that everybody has to have an ego. Jung called it the center of consciousness. Descartes' *Cogito ergo sum.* (I think therefore I am) is the best one-liner description of an ego imaginable. As soon as we can think, we enter the world of choices, the world of duality. Like Adam and Eve, we are expelled from the unconscious paradise of our infancy.

I went on to say that Erich Neumann, a friend of Jung's, called infancy the ouroboric phase, after the ouroboros, the symbolic serpent who forms a circle by swallowing its tail. When we are babies, it seems, we live in an undifferentiated state. If you watch a baby, you can see it try to focus for a little bit and then whoops! it's out to lunch, off somewhere.

It takes quite a while for the ego to form, so little kids usually start out referring to themselves in the third person. Gradually, though, they come up with the word *mine!* and shortly thereafter come the words *I* and *No!* The child begins to see that it has choices. It has entered the world of duality and consciousness, of either/or. It's as if we have eaten from the Tree of Knowledge of Good and Evil. That's two. And Adam and Eve were once one, but became two in a rather clumsy fashion. But myths always have a deeper truth, one that is important to the psyche. The longing of man and woman for each other is a metaphor for the inner longing for the mutual union of the ego and the Self, the *I* and the Divine Guest.

"You mean to say that eventually the ego gets stuck out there and forgets it has a center." You pointed to the circumference in the sand. "It's curious, but to draw a proper circle, one needs a compass or two points, one in the center and one at the circumference."

"Yes, and that proves the point!"

"So the ego is who we think we are, but not who we really are. Is that what Jung meant?"

"I really believe that's right." I described how we are given a name and we grow up identifying more and more with the temporary personality that embodies us. It's a bit like an actor playing Hamlet and never being able to get off the stage and remember that he is really Joe Blow playing at being Hamlet. "We get so used to playing the part of Alice or Walter, we forget that we can go home and have a beer—or take a break. Psychologically speaking, it's called 'identification with the ego.'

It's a heady experience and can lead to narcissism and great inflations. . . ."

"And deflations," you said, making a sad face. "I suppose both are forms of pride and thinking that we are the doers rather than the instruments. But how do you know when you are identified with your ego? Is it like the story of Mulla Nasruddin?"

"What story?"

"The one about the time he went to the bank and they asked him if he had any identification. So he took out a pocket mirror and looked into it and said, 'Yup, that's me all right.' "

"That's a new one!" I laughed. "But that's it. He identified with a reflection, not his true Self. Well," I continued, trying to be serious, "you know what I sometimes say—you can be sure that you are identified with your ego when you run out of steam and suddenly begin to define life as just one damn thing after another. You get up in the morning, brush your teeth, go to work, come home, watch TV, and go to bed, day after day, so to speak, knowing that the best you can hope for is to retire to Florida and kick the bucket. There are millions of variations on this hopeless theme. Jung describes this as a life perceived as 'nothing but . . .'. We are not leading a symbolic life, when we are that identified with our ego."

"What's a person to do?"

"Well, we are told that we do get a break from the ego in two different ways. One is when we are asleep, and another is when we meditate, which actually means 'going to the center.' But usually, it takes a crisis, a death, an illness, or a depression so deep that the person feels suicidal. Sometimes the shake-up is less traumatic, just an anxiety or a sense of utter meaninglessness to life. You see, if the ego has totally forgotten the Self, this does not mean that the Self has forgotten the ego. It, too, has its agenda. So just when things are at their worst, rescue is closest. We might suddenly think of looking for the solution within ourselves, or we may reach out for religion again, or we may turn to therapy. It seems almost as if we are meant to help one another under such circumstances."

"It makes you think of the story of the Prodigal Son in a new light," you mused. "And maybe why Jesus told the fishermen to fish on the other side."

We looked at the circle again, and at the same moment both of us came up with the Hindu and Buddhist concept of being caught on the wheel of samsara, around and around, lifetime after lifetime, until we wake up. We laughed again because so often we think the same thought simultaneously that we've decided we're halfwits!

"So what is the solution?" you wanted to know.

Carefully, I sketched a dotted line from B to A.

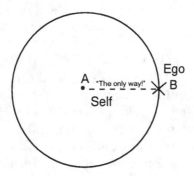

N.B. Self = center and totality of circle.

"I think this is what Jung was suggesting psychologically, and what the great Teachers have hinted at spiritually. To get from the ego back to the luminous Self is the 'Only Way.' In psychology, it is called 'establishing the ego-Self axis,' which is about as ugly a description as I can think of. Give me a poet any day! It is the reunion of the Lover with the Beloved. It is a coniunctio of utter bliss, a peak experience. To descend to the ridiculous, it's like popcorn—once you have popped you can never go back!"

"You mean the avatars popped?" You looked shocked, and then we laughed and agreed that samadhi or this blissful coniunctio must also be joyous and not without humor. If it is true in the macrocosm, it must be true in the microwave. The sacred lies well-hidden in the commonplace.

"You mean to say that that dotted line is *it*?"

We looked at it solemnly, in awe.

"That's the secret, geometrically expressed. That's it. It's like looking at a map for lost treasure, which it is. The Sufis even have a name for it: *el-tawil*. That's defined as spiritual hermeneutics or going from the outer to the inner essence of things. Mercy Muchmore—for me—calls it 'seeing with a loving eye.' "

"I guess getting from here to there really is the Only Way. It looks so simple there in the sand," you said, "but how do we do it, do you suppose?"

"We need a guide. That's where Hagia Sophia, Holy Wisdom, comes in. Remember, she goes by many names in different cultures. But for us, Sophia is called the Paraclete, the Comforter. Comforters are kind, practical, cheery presences and usually give good advice. Remember, too, that we discovered her archetype hiding out in fairy tales as the Fairy Godmother. We each have an inner guide, a personification of intuition, an inner 'godmother.' She mothers the reborn incarnation of God within each of us. After all, we can't be reborn without a mother!" I laughed. "Seriously, this must be the origin of the beautiful Virgin Birth of almost all the avatars. At one level it is an ineffable mystery, and at the human level or the simplest level, you find the Fairy Godmother. It may not make sense literally, but symbolically it makes all the sense in the world. Thinking symbolically frees us to understand the wisdom hidden within paradoxes. You know, for the child in me, it is Mercy Muchmore. Like Santa Claus, she is both real and not real. She's my personification of one of the archetypes."

"What does she recommend?" you asked quite solemnly.

"Lunch. Sandwiches and a spot of tea."

Your face lit up. "That's a very wise archetype."

We sat in the sunshine as we ate our picnic and watched the tide rise. The gentle edge of the waves began lapping closer and closer to the edge of our circle. Little by little the ring of its wisdom dissolved and slipped into oblivion to be carried out to the great ocean of the unconscious again. But the pattern remains built into each of us and into the cosmos itself, wheeling out in the solar system and whizzing about in the orbits of each atom in every molecule. God geometrizes, indeed.

We agreed to talk about the "how to do it" the next day. I felt I had to have a consultation with my inwit first to find the right words. Others might call that process prayer! Prayer is the yearning and reaching of the ego for the center of our soul.

As I write this here at Rosecroft, it is snowing. Each sparkling snowflake is a different hexagon. Each psyche is a perfect circle, all with the same contents, and no two are alike. "God is a circle whose center is everywhere and whose circumference is nowhere." As I write of the circle disappearing into the sands of Iona, I can feel the snowflakes melting in my heart. It is all one and the same.

PARADOX

How wealthy I am
in such a lack,
how rich
in the specific of poverty!
I have everything this day
but you to share it with
and so it seems I have nothing—
yet, knowing such ever-brimming loss
I am beyond my peers of need.

> *It is like having all of never*
> *into which to set a now.*

—A.O.

Without the tension between opposites of the harp string
there could be no music.

—Heraclitus

. . . That inner eye which is the bliss of solitude.

—William Wordsworth

Jung's transcendent function is not unlike the little tab
on a zipper that unites the separated sides. When we
think symbolically (symbolein—to throw together) the fabric
is made whole. When we separate the fabric, it is "diabolical"
(dia-bolein—to throw apart). The process accorded the
devil is that of separating us from truth. It's something
to remember when you zip up your pants.

—Mercy Muchmore

Behold but One in all things; it is the second that leads
you astray.

—Kabir

Love is the great Amen of the universe.

—Novalis

IV

Dark within Light, Light within Dark

The Celts have a lovely image called the *Tir-nan-Og*, the Land of Youth, the Blessed Isles, the Happy Isles. Each of us has such an island within our souls—a beautiful space within us to visit. I remember when I was a teacher of children, I assigned a composition exercise called "My Island." Without any hesitation, the children, then about ten and eleven years old, happily began imaging their island. Each made a map and peopled it according to their wishes. Animals, birds, fish, trees, mountains, and springs appeared miraculously full-blown from the unconscious of these children. It was as if they carried a paradise within them, just the right size.

The Happy Isles are an archetypal place, and I mention this, lest anyone get discouraged at the thought that they cannot travel to Scotland and the Hebrides—to Iona, the Isle of the Dove. We have our own "Iona" within us. A lovely exercise to give oneself as one is falling asleep is to image what one's Happy Isle would be like. Further, it is a lovely place to invite one's Divine Guest, the Self,

to visit. This *Tir-nan-Og* is the Celtic equivalent
of the Buddhist "Pure Land of Bliss."

The Chinese have a saying, "If you keep a green
bough in your heart, surely the singing bird will
come." And the same is true of the soul. All too
often we fill our psyches with self-incrimination,
fault-finding, and woe, and expect our Divine Guest
to walk constantly in the dungeons of our own
imprisonment. The Self comes anyway, but it must be
an awful drag! We really do have the option to invite
our Divine Guest to partake of our joys and our
sense of the beautiful. We should never lack an
inner sanctuary, a secret garden, an island of peace,
where we can visualize the Beloved walking bare-
foot. "How beautiful are the feet of him that bringeth
peace."

This concept of an inner island of beauty is free
for the taking. All we need do is image it. It is one
of the secrets of Sophia, who, it is written in scripture,
played with the Lord at the time of creation.

The miraculous thing about the outer Iona is that
it has become a collective image of a Happy Isle
for so many. People only hear the name and sigh
in wonder. I have received many letters from readers
who have read my book *The Dove in the Stone* express-
ing this very notion.

The two hundred or so indigenous inhabitants of
Iona, St. Columba's island, are actually ordinary,
sensible Scottish folk, bemused perhaps at so many
thousands of pilgrims coming to their bit of rocky
and barren terrain. But they handle it well enough
and know that much of their livelihood depends

upon it. For many visitors, though, it is as if another invisible island suffuses this one with an inner light, as if the separation between worlds is thinner here, as they say. Felix Mendelssohn felt it, as did Samuel Johnson and others in the past. Today there is a small museum in the Manse dedicated to the history of the people, the fisherfolk and farmers, who struggled for centuries to eke out a living and who suffered tremendous hardships. The restoration of the abbey, which must have been felt at one time as a surprising intrusion, has also brought a modest prosperity to the local folk. In winter, Iona returns to them, though the abbey and a few Iona Community residents remain throughout the season, and the Hotel Argyll stays open.

I believe that people are drawn to Iona to be nourished. There is magic here, and it is holy magic. They say of the island that if you are not supposed to come onto it, you will not be able to get off the boat. And there are—as in many other parts of Scotland—tales of mysterious doings and unexplainable events: sightings of ghosts of Vikings and monks, and the like.

A friend who is an Episcopal priest told me that a Scottish friend of his had been at a Sunday morning worship at the abbey several decades ago. The congregation was waiting because the minister was quite late. All of a sudden a strange man walked in the door, made his way to the altar, and proceeded to conduct the service. There were two astonishing things about this. One was that nobody knew the man, and the other was that he stood dripping wet with seaweed falling off his clothes. At the end of the service the stranger vanished, leaving only the seaweed behind. Out of curiosity, samples of this seaweed were sent to a laboratory for identification. Word came back that this species of plant came from the very deepest level of the ocean! This same Scottish friend of the priest told of going outdoors in the moonlight and feeling a strong tug pulling him toward the water. It was so strong that he had to hang on to a wall to resist it.

Since these tales are third hand, I cannot vouch for their truth, but the stories are wonderfully spooky and very Celtic. St. Columba himself was famous for having second sight, and tales of this gift abound in his biographies. One of his prophecies concerning Iona, recorded by Adamnan, certainly has come true:

> Small and mean though this place is, yet it shall be held in great and unusual honour not only by Scotic kings and people but also by foreign and barbarous nations and by their subjects; the Scots also of other churches shall regard it with no uncommon reverence.

Today there are said to be no less than forty-eight Scottish kings, eight Norwegian, and four Irish rulers buried on the island. Christianity and learning, coming from Ireland with Columba, spread out indeed through Columba's disciples. As one of the hundreds of thousands of barbarians from distant shores, I count myself fortunate to have returned again and again to this strangely compelling island.

I believe that Iona is becoming sacred to the Dove of the Holy Spirit for more and more visitors today. *Iona* means "dove" in Hebrew, and so does *Columba* in Latin. Sophia's symbol is the dove.

The wonderful work of the international Iona Community, which is centered in Glasgow and in

the abbey, spreads a spiritual light of peace throughout the world. One night we took communion in the
abbey at a long table set down the length of the
nave. It was served by a vibrant young woman, and
it was embellished on this occasion by beautiful
chanting of a prayer in Arabic by a Muslim. The
Dove tops a sculpture by Jacob Epstein in the
cloister and is inscribed with his dedication as a Jew
to the idea of universal love. This ecumenical
approach is a bold move and surely a healing for
the world.

The abbey itself, restored through the vision
and lifelong efforts of Lord Fuinary, George MacLeod,
who died only recently at the age of ninety-six, is a
testimony to a man who claimed that one should be
able to meet God in the High Street, that the Spirit
is right here in the world and among us all. This was
a new and controversial concept for the organized
church of his time, but an idea long dormant in
Celtic Christianity. "God Under my Roof" is a phrase
from a Gaelic prayer and the title of a fine commentary on Celtic Christianity by Esther de Waal.

The night after our day at the beach, I couldn't
get to sleep. Without waking you, I quietly dressed
and tiptoed out with my flashlight. The night was
soft enough, blacker than black, and wild with stars.
The only lights shining were across the sound at
Fionnphort. The island itself lay in the dark lap of
heaven. I walked past the abbey and turned left and
climbed the Hill of the Dead. I didn't have to go far
to find myself back on a spot where fifteen years
previously I had once sat in grief and despair. At

that time, it seemed as if I had come to the island only to weep.

I was torn between love and wisdom. I imagine many women can understand what I mean. To love and be loved on the personal level seems somehow so basic to joy. To become wise is a transpersonal goal, and during the thirty years since I had met my teacher M, I had become committed somehow to the deep desire to become wiser. Wisdom differs from knowledge; its source is the heart as well as the head. If I was to be of any use in this world, I knew that wisdom was essential. As I looked back at my sorrowful figure, I realized that I had then been at least wise enough to see that I was lacking in both wisdom and love! All I could do was pray that I would make the right choice between these seeming opposites.

Now, as you lay fast asleep in the hotel, I lay back on a feathery, heathery spot and searched for the Pleiades, the Big Dipper, and Orion. There were so many dancing stars, I could barely find these constellations. I knew that I am happy now, happy with a lasting joy. I am happy because I discovered that Sophia means wisdom, and that it is she whom the philosophers sought and loved. Wisdom is no longer for me a white-bearded old man, but an elusive, flirtatious, and merry Holy Spirit (sharp as a tack!), hiding in all creation, waiting for us to discover her through consciousness. We need only a consciousness developed enough to find her hidden all about by looking with a loving eye. An early myth surrounding her speaks of her hiding playfully in "drops of light" in every atom and within us in every flash of insight. Love and wisdom are one, not opposites. They are enfolded one within the other. One cannot be wise without being loving, or loving without eventually becoming wise—in the sense of knowing when to say yes and when to say no, when to stay and when to go—to learn to distinguish between limits and the limitless.

While I had been growing towards this insight, "the geometry of being" had been a help to me and a guide to better understanding symbolism. I had discovered that geometry is one of Sophia's seven pillars of wisdom. I had discovered the wonderful term "the morphology of concepts," which defines the very shapes of wisdom. It means that through pondering and contemplating the basic geometric forms, one could discover wisdom lying encoded. This was another of Sophia's games and a delightful one to play.

Shapes, of course, are delineated by lines. The straight line, according to Euclid, moves up from the no-dimension of the point to the first dimension, that of length only. When we think of opposites we usually think of a line:

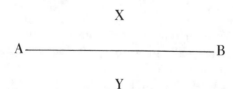

X is now separate from Y. As in the first act of creation recounted in Genesis, the light is separated from darkness, day from night. The great sequence of opposing dualities that the ancients realized were necessary for manifestation has begun.

Likewise, A is not B. B is not A. It is like a tug of war. In astronomy/astrology (another of the pillars of wisdom), the first opposite in the circle of the zodiac comes between the first sign Aries (Mars) and Libra (Venus), the Scales, between I and Thou. If you look at scales, you will see that the two pans are balanced one against the other. All the attention goes to the opposites:

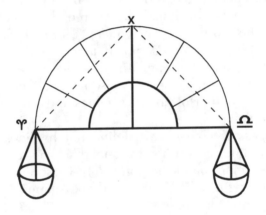

We tend to overlook the fulcrum holding the two in balance. If we call the fulcrum X, we have an equilateral triangle.

Caitlin Matthews, in her wonderful book *Sophia: Goddess of Wisdom*, gives us the three triangles of the Russian philosopher and mystic Vladimir Soloviev (1853-1900). These balance out the trinities which proceed from the One emanating into two balanced opposites:

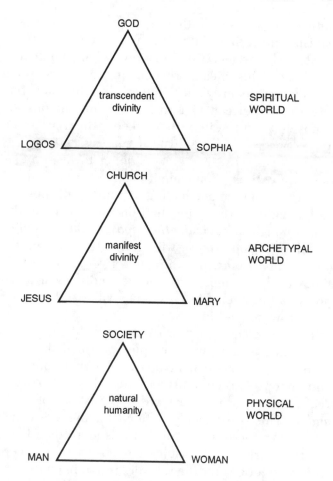

I looked at the stars again. They were winking. I remembered that Jung also used triangles. He used them to describe, among other things, the transcendent function. In his essay on the matter, he urged us all to "hang onto the opposites," to see both good and evil rather than to choose one and banish the other into the unconscious only to righteously project the "Shadow" of evil onto our neighbor. This means recognizing and accepting readily, consciously, and cheerfully the fact that one is not perfect. Get to know your demons, he counseled, and watch them, keep them in sight! When you are being selfish or spiteful or dishonest or whatever, observe yourself doing these things— don't deny them! You cannot change yourself unless you are honest about feeling at times both positive and negative. According to Jung, if one does this long enough, a *coincidentia oppositorum*, a coming together of opposites, will generate a third, the *tertium non datur*, the third not given. An apex, or the X in the triangle, will emerge, and the particular problem that seemed so insoluble will dissolve, or we may grow beyond it.

This, of course, is a gross oversimplification and has to do far more with complex personal situations than moral choices. It involves balancing conscious and unconscious contents with detached integrity. It really means using the word *and* instead of *or*: A *and* B. This is extremely difficult for the ego which must learn the bitter truth that it is more than likely far from perfect and must learn to observe and accept its imperfections for the sake of growth in consciousness. "The sun shines on the just and the unjust." Jesus reminded us to consider the lilies who neither toil nor spin, yet Solomon in all his glory was not clad like one of them. Perhaps he was reminding us that to try too hard to be good can be bad for us, that we would be much better and happier if we allowed the "goodness" of the Self to shine through us, in which case, the ego would become an instrument rather than a prideful autonomous obstacle. So the X-factor, the fulcrum, is symbolic of the reconciliation of opposites through consciousness and inner humility. The reward is greater insight and wisdom. "Know thyself."

TRANSCENDENT FUNCTION

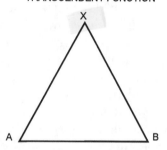

I looked forward to discussing these ideas with you and seeing what you would think of them. I looked forward to the precious days ahead. Now I rolled over and buried my face in the tickly, rough heather which was wet with dew and went on thinking.

Jung maintained that many of our outer problems are solved as we change our inner consciousness because our perception of the problem changes. We cease to cry out "If only—!" and make a change within the psyche. Personally, I have observed this to be absolutely true. I would add only one caveat. No sooner have you learned the "lesson" than— watch out! Life will test you for good measure to see that you now can apply it. Knowing the answer is not enough. That would be knowledge, not wisdom.

Wisdom is knowledge applied. I could hear M saying, "It's not yours until you can demonstrate it."

It was getting a bit chilly out there, but I had one more small shock of memory. I remembered the first time that I had lain out in a field under the stars. I was nine and was in a Swiss boarding school. My friend and I looked up at the stars and asked each other solemnly what we wanted to do when we grew up. I remember clearly that I intended to reconcile the opposites of science and religion. Though I failed to become a scientist, I believe that I found a very real potential for that reconciliation in the deepest concepts underlying astrology. It may take time for science to stop omitting the spiritual aspect of life and for science to be humble enough to acknowledge its own limitations. And the religions of the world will need to honor science heightening our consciousness of how wondrously the world of nature is constructed. This is beautifully summarized in a quotation from the anonymous and devout Christian author of *Meditations on the Tarot*:

> Now, the ideal of Hermeticism is *contrary* to that of science. Instead of aspiring to power over the forces of Nature by means of the destruction of matter, Hermeticism aspires to conscious participation with the constructive forces of the world on the basis of an alliance and a cordial communion with them. Science wants to *compel* Nature to obedience to the will of man such as it is; Hermeticism—or the philosophy of sacred magic—on the contrary wants to purify, illumine and change the will and nature of man in order to bring them into harmony with

the creative principle of Nature (*natura naturans*) and to render them capable of receiving its willingly bestowed *revelation*.

The ecological crisis today is forcing us "to change our will and nature."

One final observation came to me, as I began to shiver a little, the cool becoming cold. It had to do with the words *yoke* and *yoga* and the letter *Y*. We can yoke the opposites and use them as a team of horses or oxen to carry us onward or inwardly upward. The caduceus of Hermes, that symbol of healing and healers, is also a ladder of triangular opposites. (A circle or an oval can be bisected by two opposing triangles.) The twin serpents of the *ida* and *pingala* twist up the rod of the *shushumna* in yoga.

As long as we are in the manifest world, the principle of duality obtains. The One has to become Two, and through strife and reconciliation and love, the Two

reunite in the great dance of life. This is what the
Hindus term *lila*, the playful dance of the eternal
lovers, Radha and Krishna. I remember a striking dream concerning opposites
told to me by a client I will call Emma. I asked her
to write it down:

I am walking through the paved square of a university
campus. Off to the side is a table at which a Tibetan
lady sits with some students. She beckons to me and
invites me to join them. The Tibetan lady is dressed
in native costume, and she has black hair parted in
the middle and bound in a bun in the back. She has a
charming, ageless face, but I know that she is much
older than she looks. The Tibetan lady now tells the
following tale:
"I once met a Tibetan lama who told me that he
had had the following dream: 'I dreamt,' said he, 'that
I was chanting *om mani padme hum*, and when I came
to the chorus of prayers, I heard wind chimes, the
tinkling sound of bells, and the sweet voices of
children singing. And I looked up and down and
to the right and to the left and saw no one and
nothing there.' "
As the Tibetan lady told this, I myself, heard the
sound of wind chimes, tinkling bells, and the sweet
voices of children. So I asked the Tibetan lady if she
realized that these lovely sounds accompanied her
story, and that I, too, had looked up and down, to
the left and to the right, and had seen nobody nor
nothing there. The Tibetan turned to me with a special
radiant smile, looked at me knowingly, and gave me
a big wink.
The Tibetan lady next asked the students to close
their eyes and imagine a glowing sun. When I closed
my eyes I saw a glowing, golden sphere out of which,
surprisingly, radiated two wide beams of light. The

one on the left was pure gold. The one on the right was silvery blue and held upon it, like a landscape for a toy train, mountains, lakes, trees, animals, houses, cars, and thousands of people, busy at their lives. When I described this to the Tibetan lady, she said, "That's exactly right. Now, you must remember that in your dimension they seem to be two and you feel you have to make a choice. What is important to realize is that, whichever one you choose, in reality they both are One." I knew, even in the dream, that one could not choose one without choosing the other. This dream seemed real, more like a true experience than a dream. It has so many levels of reality enfolded within each other, I know that I will be working on understanding it for many years to come.

Still under the spell of the memory of Emma's vision, I crept back shivering to the backdoor of the hotel, which I had left off the latch—down the hall and quietly into our room. You still slept as a polar bear would sleep, the Sound of Iona slept silver in the starlight. The boats rocked, and the gulls and the sheep and the cows and the children and all of the island called me back to trust and gratitude. I slipped back into bed and reached out and touched your warm hand just to be sure I hadn't dreamt it all.

And all the while, I knew Sophia was out there dancing under the stars.

SONNET

Euclid alone has looked on Beauty bare.
Let all who prate of Beauty hold their peace,
And lay them prone upon the earth and cease
To ponder on themselves, the while they stare
At nothing, intricately drawn nowhere
In shapes of shifting lineage; let geese
Gabble and hiss, but heroes seek release
From dusty bondage into luminous air.
O blinding hour, O holy, terrible day,
When first the shaft into his vision shone
Of light anatomized! Euclid alone
Has looked on Beauty bare. Fortunate they
Who, though once only and then but far away,
Have heard her massive sandal set on stone.
                              —Edna St. Vincent Millay

Where could I stray to, where?
This point is my centre . . .
With this earth and this ocean
To rise to the infinite:
One ray more of the sun.

                              —Jorge Gillen

The emblem of the perfect Man, says Monoïmus, is the jot
or tittle. This one tittle is the uncompounded, simple,
unmixed Monad, having its composition from nothing
whatsoever, yet composed of many forms, of many parts.
That single, indivisible jot is the many-faced, thousand-eyed
and thousand-named, the jot of the iota. This is the emblem
of that perfect and indivisible Man. . . . The Son of the Man
is the one iota, the one jot flowing from on high, full and
filling all things, containing in himself everything that is
in the Man, the Father of the Son of Man.
                              —Hippolytus

V

Filling the Cup

Overnight the weather changed. We woke to pouring rain and gale force winds. The windows rattled and braced themselves, and outside the mountains of Mull and Fionnphort suddenly vanished, as the waves of the Sound raced southward full of white caps. At breakfast, it became known that the ferry would not run and had already sailed around the corner of Mull to take refuge from the storm. Most of the guests opted for a book in the lounge, or they tackled the postcards that they had promised to send off. There was a warm coziness in the room and the deep silence one associates with the British love of reserve. We had noticed that when the American groups came and went, their high-pitched chatter and laughter became deafening, if not embarrassing.

Since we had an errand to do at Finlay & Ross, the small dry goods store, we thought it might be an adventure to head out into the weather. So on with our wellies and our slickers, and out we went. Neither of us can be called skinny; hefty would be a better word. But despite our weight, the wind tried to push us up the walls. It snatched away our laughter, and I had to hang onto Woodstock for dear life. The rain was not wet; it was cold and juicy and dribbled down our faces. We passed several patient dripping sheep and a dog whose ears were almost blown off his head. By the time we reached the shop and burst in the door, we were soaked, but triumphant. A grand ruffling of recent newspapers announced our entrance, and all the picturesque dish towels hung up for sale from the ceiling waved like banners to welcome us. I bought some ink cartridges, and you bought some shaving cream. The woman behind the counter shook her head and deplored the weather. "It's terrrrrible just!" she exclaimed, rolling her *rs* in a way that would take me weeks to master.

The Martyrs Bay Restaurant across the street seemed a good place to go next for a hot cup of tea and a scone or two. The place was empty, and we found a nice table by the window with a view out to sea and of the waves crashing against the jetty.

The tea was hot and strong, and we sat together and relaxed, feeling that we had earned it. But you must picture that throughout the following conversation, squalls of rain continued to dash against the windows, and a distant roar of wind and sea rose and fell, shuddering the building. It was entirely grand— Scottish weather at its best.

"I've been thinking a lot about Sophia's games, as you call them—the hide-and-seek of wisdom and the joy with which you ferret them out. How did you come upon the idea in the first place? Was it something you read?" you began.

"No. It's a strange story. Perhaps it's hard to believe,

but it is true." I reminded you that I waded through many, many books and scriptures of all the religions from the time that I was twelve until I was twenty, always looking for something that could tell me what was meant by the word *God*. It was as if all these books were telling me about the way it is supposed to be, but they did not bring me closer to any personal experience that could serve as proof.

I did experience one exception in Belgium the summer I was twelve. I read in a science book given to me by my father that the world is made up of atoms, and the atoms are made up of energy. I had a sudden revelation. Perhaps that universal energy itself is God! The thought was so tremendous that I literally shook all over. I ran blindly out of my bedroom in the hotel. I looked down the open stairwell at the bald pate of the concierge and wanted to shout at him, "Guess WHAT!" But then I realized that there was nobody I could talk to. So I didn't.

I decided at that point that some of the Bible stories I had been told could not be literally true. Like many other people, who reach this pass, I decided I must be an atheist. It took many, many more years before I discovered that almost all religious stories are true—but true of the psyche. Reading them symbolically restored them to my heart.

I told you the Hindu story about a youth who, seeking to become a chela of a guru, asked the master if he could be his disciple. The guru looked at him and beckoned him to the village well. There he seized the youth by the neck, and held his head under the water, almost drowning him. When the sputtering youth inquired in shock why the guru had done this, the guru replied, "When you want

God as badly as you did your next breath, come back to me."

"Well," I continued, "I had reached that point in New York, when I was twenty-one [as I have recounted in a previous book *Jungian Symbolism in Astrology*.] Fate intervened. I not only met Hermes, my first astrology teacher, but on the very next day I met his teacher M." Taking another swig of tea, I reminisced. I reminded you how M, a vigorous and wonderful man in his seventies with white hair, pink cheeks, and a presence like no other, took charge. He invited me to his "lab" as he called it, which was in the flat below that of Hermes, in an old house on Prince Street, a house that I have described as always smelling of Clorox and roses.

M sat me down and queried me about my quest. Then he talked to me of John Dee and Dalton. I was amazed at the courtesy and respect with which he spoke to me. I sensed that he looked deep into my soul and saw that I was earnest. I felt as if I had come home. In all the years I knew him subsequently, he never failed to impress me and others with his strength, common sense, and dignified reserve. He never spoke of himself; his only concern was for those who turned to him for guidance. The odd thing was that he rarely gave advice directly. He brought you up to a point where you would have your own attack of insight. Then he would twinkle. The most valuable lesson that he taught me was that behind every event in our lives is a purpose, and it is up to us to discover it. This means paying attention. Almost fifty years have passed since I met him. I still love him with all my heart. He changed my life forever.

I told you how that night I returned to the Hotel Holley on Washington Square, where I was staying with my parents. We had returned from Europe because of the war, since my father could no longer do business for his company over there.

That night, I woke up suddenly with an urge to write. I got out of bed for a pad and a pencil and a box of puffed rice to snack on. I sat in my nightie on my bed, and the words just flowed onto the paper. The words were about the philosophical importance of geometry. The message was that step by step one could use geometry as a proof for the existence of what I was seeking. Even now I get excited recalling that the proof I sought was right under my nose, everywhere about, but that I had to learn *how* to play the game to find it.

To this day, I told you, I feel that most of us experience life as a game that we are born to play, but no one gives us the rules of how to play it. I don't mean moral or ethical rules, but the instructions of how to look and see and find the other world that is hidden in this one.

You nodded your head sagely and ordered another cup of tea. "What were the rules, then?"

I paused to open a little packet of demerara sugar to add to my tea, even though it's supposed to go with coffee.

"Well, the first step was to realize that everything we see around us and all that we experience are potentially our teachers. We see only half of anything: the whole consists of adding the meaning to what we see. As with any cube, you only see three sides, yet you know that it has six. *You* supply the hidden ones to make it whole."

I remembered a drawing that came that night. I sketched it for you on my paper napkin.

I showed that by adding the two halves, you generated a third, which could become the half of something else, and so on and on.

Understanding something functions like ripples on a pond around a dropped stone. They keep on spreading out. It made me see raindrops differently as their small circles spread out and interweave with each other. Consciousness does the same. Hindus use that very image in describing the *samskaras*, the disturbances of a mind that is not still.

"To sum it up," I went on, "there seem to be four steps in learning Sophia's game—no, I did not know about Sophia then—they are:

1) To look.

2) To actively notice.

3) To draw any logical conclusion from what you observe. Science does this, but there it stops because that is the limit science puts upon itself.

4) *To connect what you have noticed to any possible spiritual implication it might have.* This science does not do, nor, by and large, does organized religion, which seems to have lost the key to symbolic thinking. The rituals may continue, but the deeper understanding of the actual objects used ritually is almost never taught. In Christianity the great schisms over the hypostatic union of Christ or the transubstantiation of bread and wine into the body and blood of Jesus are today mainly philosophical arguments or are required beliefs and dogma for the faithful. The debate continues, but the symbolic import underlying the questions and the psychological needs they meet are rarely grasped. Just ask around."

I had to confess to you that the depth of symbolic meaning available in the Roman Catholic mass came alive for me only through reading Jung's "Transformation Symbolism in the Mass," and he was born a Protestant! I begged you to read it when we got home.

"Do you mean that the reason we do not understand the rituals of religions is because we have not connected to their symbolic meaning through personal experience?" you asked.

"Yes, exactly. We mostly haven't bothered, and our teachers may never have known. Jung's father was a pastor. He confessed to his son that he really did not know what he was doing, he only had faith. This struck Jung as a tragic situation. It probably set him off on his own quest to know rather than to believe."

Getting back to "The Geometry of Being" which was precipitating for me that night in the hotel (and which continued for months), I told you that naturally I was curious and excited by what I was learning. I went to M and asked him what was going on, but he only smiled enigmatically and twinkled. He just suggested that I keep it up.

I learned a lot about geometry and later about the symbolic nature of colors and numbers. It was even more exciting as time went by, and I discovered that other people had written on similar themes and what they wrote checked out with what I was setting down. But for myself the proof lay in the fact that what I was learning was already stashed away somewhere in my unconscious. I honestly did not take it in; it came out. It set me on a joyous course for life. Years later, when I discovered that Sophia's way of teaching is one of joy in wisdom, not of heaviness, I longed to share the idea. But I had to wait almost twenty years before I could teach. Marriage and four children came in between.

I found that children excel at playing these games, and so do poets. The Chinese, at least in olden times, used to train their children in basic observation, as Ernest Wood pointed out in his excellent little book *Concentration.* In it, he tells how Chinese children were given a piece of jade and asked to enumerate as many qualities as they could discover in it. In my work with young students, I placed an added emphasis on process, that is the verb that might be hidden in the object. This is how I eventually discovered "the Dove in the stone," the Dove being Sophia or wisdom hidden in matter.

I found that some of my older students, for instance, would connect a cup or glass to the chalice in church, or the Holy Grail to mythic cauldrons and even to the soul as container, or the Mother Goddess as the physical container of life as form.

"That's amazing," you exclaimed softly.

"The funny thing is that hardly anybody remembers to look for the frozen verb—the process. Symbolically speaking, what is a cup doing?"

"Containing," you said with a grin, sloshing your teacup around. "Just like my stomach!"

Over the years I discovered that you could connect the answers people gave with Jung's four basic typologies. The sensation types wrote down words which, when put together, helped you to know it was a cup. The feeling types made judgments. The thinking types were more interested in the origins and form of the cup. And just to tease, the intuitives —who were the quickest to reach the higher symbolic levels of cupness—set down words that would leave you gasping, *breast, womb, imagination, nature, emptiness.* No one would ever guess they were referring to a plain old cup! The intuitives had no problem filling in the gaps. They saw all those items as capable of holding or containing contents, of having the capacity to be filled, to store, and to give out again.

We watched a gull out the window, stationary in mid-air as it attempted to fly against the wind. It was soon joined by another. Behind them we could see the spume blowing off the top of the dark grey waves.

You spoke. "I suppose the importance of any such game of Sophia's is that you experience the archetypal nature of the process for yourself. I can see that when you realize the feminine nature and function of containing, you can see that behind the great Western myth of the search for the Holy Grail lies the search for the lost feminine, for Sophia. You know, in the German version of the story, the Dove came every year on Good Friday to renew the power of the Grail, so the connection is implicit. It is the Chalice, or in Celtic mythology the cauldron, that holds the Spirit (wine) or the Truth or Immortality. Our bodies and the entire manifest and visible world are given form by the feminine—by mothers and Mother Nature. To me, this really makes sense."

We looked down thoughtfully at our heavy china teacups and for a second appreciated them as holy vessels in disguise.

There was another huge gust of wind and rain against the window, but we were safely contained in the womb of the room in which we sat so companionably. The clouds were lifting from the water now and scudding over the lower mountains like ships in full sail. The scene was dramatic and filled with moiling energy.

"How would you express Sophia's game geometrically?" you asked.

"With the circle we drew on the beach. The ego sitting at the circumference is constantly dealing with both the outer and the inner of the psyche. By engaging in contemplation, it learns through ingestion. When it doesn't take the time for this, it just goes round and round not comprehending. It's a bit like conception, and the ancient philosophers called the lively or quickening word, the *logos spermatikos*. In common language, we even use the expression 'I couldn't conceive such a notion.' Any attack of insight or Aha! is like a little pook of conception."

"A little what?"

"Pook," I said shyly. "It was the best way that I could explain it to M. It made him laugh."

"I can just imagine," you agreed. "But if we get a bigger and bigger circle, won't we automatically get a swelled head?" you went on to tease.

"No, because the bigger the circle, the more the circumference is exposed to the unknown. So the wiser you get, the more you know you don't know! And if you are really wise, perhaps, you know that how much you know doesn't matter. Understanding even a little is more important than knowing a lot. I had to learn that the hard way."

A pleasant aroma of frying haddock wafted out of the kitchen. It was almost lunchtime. Now other folk were coming in and the windows steamed up rapidly. I always enjoy watching people, and these were wonderful to observe. Old women with crocheted woolen caps over their white hair, stout in their coats, accompanied by sharp faced daughters and piping children struggling to get out of their mackintoshes. Little cheeks like apples, and everybody looking as if they had stepped out of a children's book: Two gawky fisherlads in navy blue wearing green boots. A solitary philosopher in a tweed coat and a tartan scarf smoking his pipe and looking distinguished with a copy of a book by Camus sticking out of his pocket. The room filled with life. The storm had done its best, but nothing could dampen the spirits of the good people on Iona.

Imagine a circle and in the middle of it a center; and from this center forthgoing radii-rays. The farther these radii go from the center, the more divergent and remote from one another they become; conversely, the nearer they approach to the center, the more they come together among themselves. Now suppose that this circle is the world: the very middle of it, God; and the straight lines (radii) going from the center to the circumference, or from the circumference to the center, are the paths of life of men. And in this case also, to the extent that the saints approach the middle of the circle, desiring to approach God, do they, by so doing, come nearer to God and to one another. . . . Reason similarly with regard to their withdrawing from God . . . they withdraw also from one another, and by so much as they withdraw from one another do they withdraw from God. Such is the attribute of love: to the extent that we are distant from God and do not love Him, each of us is far from his neighbor also. If we love God, then to the extent that we approach to Him through love of Him, do we unite in love with our neighbors; and the closer our union with them, the closer is our union with God also.

—Avva Dorotheus (Seventh Century Greek Orthodox)

This feminine wisdom is of loving participation. Sophia is living and present and near, a godhead that can always be summoned and is always ready to intervene.

—Erich Neumann

I have a distinct feeling that number is a key to the mystery— [of the unus mundus where there is no incommensurability between so-called matter and so-called psyche]—since it is just as much discovered as invented. We define number psychologically as an archetype of order that has become conscious.

—C. G. Jung

Every soul is centered in her intelligent part, where she is truly and most fully one; but because of her plurality she traverses a circle in her desire to embrace the Nous within herself.

—Proclus

VI
Getting the Point

Late that same evening, the storm lifted and flew away, leaving behind a dazzled fresh-washed world. The Sound turned dark navy blue, with white horses still galloping across the waters. The pink rock of Mull turned orange in the setting sun, and the wet grass glistened out the windows in an eerie golden green. The spectacle was so extraordinary that all of us in the dining room of one accord put down our soup spoons and napkins and streamed out to stand and marvel. The sun was setting in a divine epiphany. Its rays bathed the abbey, the haycocks, and the rolled-up towers of cloud in the distance, and seemed to turn everything to gold. The air glistened and sparkled. Heaven and earth seemed one.

I looked at the rapt faces of our fellow guests and the young students who waited on us. A collective sigh went up as the shadow of oncoming night slowly crept up the shore beyond, until the russet light fell only on the tip of Ben More. Then with a final kiss it was gone. Stunned, we turned and went back to our meal. I can never forget the quality of that experience. It still fills me with awe. Somehow, it made St. John's visions of heaven on Patmos, described in the Book of Revelations, seem almost plausible. Space itself had become palpably golden.

We resumed our conversation over a postprandial coffee in the lounge. You looked so handsome in the wool twill trousers we had bought in Portee the previous year. They went perfectly with the grey tweed jacket. I looked at you admiringly with much connubial affection. You looked up and teased me. You are ever the practical one.

"If you were to teach this game of Sophia's, how would you go about it?"

"I suppose I would get a blank notebook, a compass, a right angle, and a ruler."

"That sounds more like school to me." You looked anxious. "Or becoming a Mason."

"Remember Mondayschool? That's different. Sophia is the teacher, and she is already within you. All you have to do is draw her out with your drawing! And who knows but what the early Masons were on to her."

"Well, it might be worth the experiment. It's always a good excuse to go back to Finlay and Ross."

So back we went the next day and, in short order, purchased the necessary equipment. They had only one right angle, but we agreed to share. I knew I had learned some of the basic concepts of sacred geometry, but applying them inwardly and sym- bolically after fifty years would be a prayerful undertaking.

"Where shall we start?" you asked.

"I think in St. Oran's Chapel," I replied. "Since

it is a sacred undertaking, we probably should invoke the Divine Guest and Sophia, don't you think?" You cheerfully agreed.

It was only a short walk from the hotel to the chapel, and to get there, we passed the graves of Macbeth and the Norwegian and Scottish kings. The beautiful medieval grave slabs are no longer there, though they were there when I first went to Iona. The weather was wearing them away, and so they were removed to a small museum to the left of the abbey.

We reached the small chapel, the oldest structure still standing on Iona. In it there is a large bare stone altar with a simple brass cross on the wall above it. Two grave slabs flank two wooden benches and two prie-dieux. We sat down to meditate. I could almost hear Mercy Muchmore chuckling. "Did you say 'meditate?' What does the word actually mean?" It comes from the Latin *meditere* and means to go to the center. "Aha!" snorted Mercy Muchmore. "When you're in a muddle, go to the middle. That's the *only way!*"

This is the kind of thing that happens with Sophia energy. Just when you are getting a solemn face, she cracks it up with a joke. I did try to pray, but all I could see was the circle on the beach. And I saw the beach hard and smooth and empty, and I knew what the first exercise would be.

After St. Oran's, we walked up to the abbey itself. We never tire of just walking about in it. The spirit of Columba somehow is embedded there and, in fact, on the whole island. The impact that this man had upon the world is immeasurable. His disciples and theirs, in turn, spread learning back across a Europe suffering the Dark Ages between the fifth and ninth centuries.

Columba was an Irish Celt, tutored by Druids as well as early Irish Christians, so he formed a bridge between the old and the new. The Celtic Christians' tradition never rejected nature, so Sophia lived on for them as St. Brigid, the Christianized version of the goddess Brid—goddess of flocks, poetry, wisdom, and laughter. What a lovely combination!

We paid our respect to the Dove in the cloister and to the live doves outside in the sunken garden and herb garden, lovingly tended by the young people of the Community.

Finally, in our bedroom you pinned me to the task. You got out the plastic bag containing our school supplies.

"Where do we start?" you asked.

"On the first blank page. Leave it blank."

"That's it?"

"That's it."

"The first meditation is on emptiness. *Blank* means white. White light contains all the colors undifferentiated."

"It's a bit scary," you said looking down at the empty page. "I wonder if God was as afraid that He might goof up as I am."

"In the beginning. . . . Beginning anything is scary. Perhaps there isn't any beginning. Only the ego-mind insists on beginnings and ends. Something, anything! Well, let's contemplate and see if anything comes."

So we did.

As I contemplated the page, I could not help but see William Blake's awesome picture, "The Ancient of Days," which suggests that the same problem confronted the Creator. I was struck at that moment by the one circle out of which the Ancient of Days leaned with the two points of the compass, his body suggesting the third line of a triangle.

I wondered, as well, if contemplating emptiness makes one question what it might symbolize, and above all what verb or process it might imply. I wondered if such a void suggests infinity. I remembered struggling as a child to conceive of limitless space or limitless time and finally giving up. Well, there's a good reason for my frustration: the ego as center of consciousness can think only in terms of duality. The mind has to choose to think this or that, either/or. It can use the word *infinity* but it cannot experience it. Somehow the mind needs a beginning before the before or some place in which to put space. The mind is the wrong instrument for contemplating this and therefore should be excused and disqualified. So the blankness or emptiness remains a mystery. This is the price we pay for being conscious. Even the word *con-scious* implies "knowing with." With whom? Me and my Self?

My thoughts moved on to consider that for some, the emptiness represents "isness" or the ground of being or not-being. It is the blank page that carries the printed words in a book. It speaks to the scary feeling that confronts the writer or the artist. It begs for creation. For this reason so many creation myths begin with the words, "In the beginning the world was void and without form." And then a god begins creation. There are two basic patterns to the process: either the god creates the universe and remains transcendent to it, as in the Old Testament; or the god divides himself in two, male and female of all species, and engenders the world through love. Here the god is implicitly immanent. The Big Bang theory is a sort of *ex nihilo* eruption into being, but it does not seem to take the idea of consciousness into account.

I saw my son in my mind's eye, aged about five, struggling with the biblical account of creation. He stood there in the kitchen, feet apart, big brown eyes challenging me. "But, Mother, if God made the world, who made God?" The discussion went in circles, as it always does, but I had an inkling that he might grow up interested in philosophy, and he did. He majored in the subject at Stanford. The best I could do on that occasion was to draw him a lemniscate:

I recalled that years later, I discovered the joys of the Moebius strip and took to writing two-line poems that go around and around. I just took a twenty-four inch strip of shopping tape, gave it one twist, and pasted the edges together. Then I wrote something like this that goes on and on and on without stopping:

> *I am everything—a unique universe—a constellium of thoughts pulled through the node of experience emerging as the one and only—not at all—I am nothing, but a handful of ashes blown away by the winds of time—I am everything—etc.*

To ask about infinity leads but to a speculative tautology: we go around and around. For this reason, perhaps, the earliest symbol we have for this mystery, historically speaking, is the empty circle itself. It tokens Spirit Unmanifest—nothing and all, all and nothing. The ancients knew that it is hard to imagine anything that a circle could not encompass. For the human psyche it is the most perfect of symbols for the *imago dei* or the image of God that we can think of. Jung gave it the Sanskrit term *mandala.* He proposed that when people dreamt of something circular, it indicated the potential wholeness or individuation of the dreamer. It is a symbolic token from the Self. We even project the value outwardly in the pearl of great price or the golden coin—the lost and buried treasure is an archetypal representation for the lost center within us.

You broke into my thoughts at just that moment, as if you had heard them. "Isn't the circle a related idea?" you asked. So for our second contemplation, we considered this:

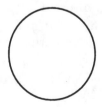

It made me think now of Lao Tzu's words:

The thirty spokes of a wheel are made one
in the hole at the hub.
It is this emptiness that furthers the wheel.
When we use clay to make a pot
it is the hollow space that makes it a pot.
Doors and windows in a house
function through this emptiness.
Thus we are using what is not
to help us use what is.

The mystery is the unknown at the center, but it is the circumference that makes it possible for the ego to deal with the mystery—at least there is something there. And if, symbolically speaking, the ego is at the circumference, it also accounts for our sense of identity and separateness. We even speak of "needing our own space." A god without a circumference can only be an abstraction, but as a poetic image, it is very moving. If God's center is everywhere, then that means what it says: the divine ipso facto is centered in you and me and in all life, in every atom.

Even this circle, which we were contemplating remains a symbol of the unknown because, as the ancient Egyptians discovered, the area of a circle can never be known. This is because the nature of pi never, ever works out evenly. The latest computer carried it out to 480,000,000 decimal places. Had the numbers been printed out, they would have stretched over six hundred miles. So what we hold in front of our eyes, and what we could swear we see totally, remains unknown—a hypothesis, at best. It is reflected perhaps symbolically in our physical vision itself. Each of us has a "blind spot." We cannot see everything. Our humility should be built in. But—and here's the beautiful logic of it all—if we can find our own center, we can find God within us.

I always feel a little embarrassed speaking about God, because the word itself means so much and so little to different people. This is why Jung always chose the words *imago dei*, the image of God. "The Tao that can be described is not the Tao." For me, the verb or process I associate with divinity is that of creating, the urge of life itself to come into being. And insofar as humankind cocreates we are made in the image of God.

As I turned these ideas over in my mind and soul, I realized I was at that very instant creating. Even as I breathe, I am in a sense creating. Sophia as Holy Spirit is also Holy Breath. The word *spirit* comes from *spirare*, to breathe.

You pointed out that the circle for prehistoric humankind was the sun which gave these people life and light and warmth. So the conflation sun and God was natural and not to be questioned. We could say that the empty circle is a reference to what the alchemists called "the Sun behind the sun," the mystery of mysteries.

You continued, "I suppose you could say that as the sun is to the solar system, so the Self is to the psyche, or the heart is to the body. It's the source of everything, of life itself. And gold never tarnishes. It all fits together, doesn't it? I can see why people thought of God as the sun, and since it is way up there in the sky, you can see why they would think that God dwelt way up there somewhere beyond the clouds in heaven. It's perfectly logical. I suppose it's what Jung would call projection."

"Projection by the ego," I interrupted with some excitement, as I felt a big insight coming up. "To the ego, the Godself has to be somewhere else. It knows that instinctively. By the same token, you could say that the whole story of the Fall and Redemption is true of the ego." "

"But Christ told us that the kingdom of heaven is within. That was a big hint, for sure," you added thoughtfully. "Perhaps we weren't ready for that yet—or only a few were. You know that radius you drew on the beach? The Only Way? I've been thinking about that. It makes the first line between two points —the center and the circumference. Going out from the center, then, it describes the Fall of the ego into duality. But we have to return in the same way inside of ourselves, and that's the Redemption of the ego. Once this has happened, we are ready for the next step."

"Which is?"

"Functioning more consciously with the Divine Guest, serving the Light at the center within us. It seems so simple looked at that way, but what a painful journey it can be!"

We now stood among the graves of Reilig Oran and looked out to the Sound. The sunlight was twinkling drops of gold off the water, and the gold was reflected even in the puddles here and there still left over from the storm. I wondered if our souls were not like puddles, too, capable of mirroring the source of light within us when our hearts are at peace. It was curious to think how the blazing fire of the sun is transmuted to light by the coolness of water. I wondered if it is the atmosphere that gives our planet a heaven filled with light. Seen from the moon and outer space, the sky is velvety black.

We returned to our room and our notebooks. Next we drew a circle with a point in it.

"Once the circle is drawn with a point in the middle, a whole new development is at hand," I mused. You nodded. "It becomes focused and represents Spirit Manifest. Even today, it is the symbol for our physical sun in astronomy and for the precious metal gold. It has become a fertile egg, so to speak."

Now we had something new to study. A single point. The great affirmative, the "yes" that comes before a "no" can sound. I chuckled when I thought of the exclamation mark, a line leading us to a point being made:

!

Aha! as Mercy Muchmore would say. So we turned a page and devoted it to this:

●

"I call the point the Hamlet syndrome," I explained. "It seems to be saying, 'To be or not to be, that is the question!' When it sits there all by itself, it is making the most profoundly cataclysmic statement possible, 'Behold, here I am!' In fact, that little point is probably the most important symbol of all, so we should look at it with awe and respect. It has led us from non-being into non-dimension—the dimension of very existence. By Euclid's definition, 'A point is that which has no parts or any magnitude.' "

We agreed that psychologically speaking, we could say the point is the starting place for the ego's understanding of unity. To draw a circle with a compass, you have to place a point somewhere. A compass has two legs; one remains stationary and the other moves. So the manifest world requires two to tango. The stillpoint at the center lives in *no dimension*, just as the Self within us dwells constantly beyond time and space, in the world that is ever hidden within *this* world. Here time is called synchronicity, and space is called a *temenos*, a sacred precinct, a space out of space.

Lest we get too muddled by this, we are familiar already with timeless time and spaceless space in our dreams. When I mentioned this, you asked for an example. So I told you of a dream I once had, one of the few with a plot—a beginning, a middle, and an end—as well as a setting. It also had a strange consequence in real life. You prudently took an apple off the windowsill and lay back on the bed crunching it, while I shared with you the following dream:

> I am sitting in the balcony of an opera house looking at the closed red velvet curtain. I glance at the program in my lap and read the title of the ballet to

come. It is in French and reads "La Danse Inter-rompu," the interrupted dance. The orchestra is warming up.

Next, the conductor comes out, the audience is hushed. He raises his baton and a loud dissonant chord sounds. The curtains open, but nobody appears on the stage. The conductor shakes his head bemused and tries again. This time the chord is in a different key. Two dancers come out, a young man and woman dressed in yellow and green. They dance beautifully, and it is obvious to us all in the audience that they are personally deeply in love with one another.

The two separate, going to opposite ends of the stage. As they turn reaching for each other, that awful chord sounds! It freezes the lovers. The orchestra stops playing. The conductor leaves the podium, followed by the entire orchestra. The audience, including me, is horrified.

Suddenly from the back of the hall a short white-haired man with a violin gets up and begins to play a melody of such incomparable sweetness that it melts the dancers. They now dance to a slow swinging waltz, back into each other's arms. I am so moved that tears run down my face, and I see that the audience is also weeping for joy. When I awake my pillow is wet. My first thought was for the beautiful music—how could I remember it? Would I ever forget it?

I looked at you and saw that you too were affected. In its way the dream had been prophetic, because I had not met you when I dreamt it.

"And did you ever find the music again?" you asked.

"Two years passed. I moved out of the house I was living in and into a reconstructed pigsty, literally. It had been a small shed for pigs. It was on an estate and measured ten by twenty feet. I renamed it "The

Dovecot." On the first day, I moved my radio into place, plugged it in, and turned it on. Out came the very same music I had heard in the dream! I dropped everything and stayed glued waiting to find out what it was."

"And did you?"

"Yes. It was Anton Dvorak's *Romance in F Minor.*"

"That's incredible," you said, and I had to agree. But it was a good demonstration of what the unconscious can whip up in the way of an alternate reality. Out of nowhere, and occupying no space or comparable time, the opera house, stage, orchestra, program, audience, and protagonists of the dream had manifested themselves. The music was the greatest mystery of all. I can only presume that I had heard it somewhere before, though I have no conscious memory of it.

In anyone's dreams, the unconscious can whip up whole landscapes, city streets, shops with all the contents displayed, people, animals—a whole theater of effects—and yet it all happens within the dreamer. Where is that space that is no space, so real and seemingly three-dimensional? The same is true for inner dreamtime. Scientific studies show that a seemingly long sequence of events can take place in a dream within a minute or even a few seconds.

I told you that I suspect the dreamworld is a clue to the time and space in which the Self lives and to which, presumably, we return after death. It is always *here* and *now* at the centerpoint. The Self, according to Jung, dwells in the unconscious. The ego cannot know it fully and live. What a paradox! "Man cannot see God and live." The best the ego can do is to observe the effects of the Self or Divine Guest, to honor its being, and experience it as ineffable. We cannot live in or on a dimensionless point, and yet without a point, there could be no lines, planes, or the solids of the outer world of three dimensions. We went on to remember that in Hinduism, our point has a name—the *bindu*. It represents the cosmic axis and is considered feminine, an aspect of Shakti (Sophia) and consciousness. It is where Shiva and Shakti, the masculine and feminine, become one. It is frequently a focus for meditation. If you think about it, the point, the stillpoint, is where all the axes of dimensions intersect. It is the point, the starting point, for manifestation to begin. No wonder Sophia has to be present. It is she, after all, who is hiding in the world in drops or points of light. And this kind of crazy geometry is one of the clues to finding her, both in the world and within ourselves.

In the Jewish Kabbalah, the point is called the *Yod*. It is the first letter in the tetragrammaton IHVH (Jahweh) and also of the Hebrew word IChIDH (Yekhidah). The letter is said to represent the coniunctio of *Kether*, the Supreme Self, the Indivisible One, with *Chokmah*, Wisdom (Sophia). So for the mystic, the point represents the union or coniunctio within of the individual with the "I Am" of creation.

We agreed that it was fascinating how so many different cultures came up with the same basic notions. Was this the result, you wondered, of the transmigration of peoples? This gave me a great opportunity to trot out the term Jung used, *autochthonic origin*, meaning "coming out of one's own depths." As I reminded you mischievously, the Self seems to speak a lot of Greek and Latin. Whenever you read Jung's works, you have to watch out for these terms, because they have implications behind implications. As my friend, Edward C. Whitmont, once remarked, "Jung's books are double-bottomed."

Anatomically speaking, you pointed out, the process is repeated in conception. Through the union of sperm and egg, we start out as one cell, which divides into two, four, sixteen, and on and on in the miracle of embryonic development.

To which I add that psychologically, then, this process points to the longed-for coniunctio of the ego with the Self, the melting in love of one with the other, once the seeker is reunited with the one sought.

At this point, we had exhausted our poor brains, and so we changed the subject to another one dear to our hearts—speculating what each of our children was doing, and how the grandchildren were showing signs of being fascinating individuals in their own right. We wondered if they would think we were round the bend, giving so much thought to points and lines. "What's the point?" they might tease. But, then, we were on Iona. It's safer there than most places to stick your toes in other dimensions.

That night we lay side by side in bed in the dark, our hands joined like children's. You spoke softly. "When we were married, we were told in the wedding ceremony that as man and woman we would become one flesh. So the same thing must happen inside of us, in our souls. We help each other to get there. I think I'm beginning to get the point!"

We laughed and rolled over and went to sleep.

Whence come these mathematical objects [i.e. points, lines, planes, and all their derivatives]? . . . they issue from the mind itself, being 'projected' by it from the inner store of forms that constitute its essence. The mind is 're-minded' of these ideas by sense perception, and its thinking is an "unfolding" [explication] of their content under guidance of a higher and fully unified intelligence.

—Glenn R. Morrow

I bow to the Goddess who is the Soul of all Yantras.

—Lalitasahasrnama

We must not consider that the circle, triangle and square are simply forms, but elements representing the divine grammar of Nature.

—Samuel Coleman

Mandala means circle . . . the basic motif is the premonition of a centre of personality, a kind of central point within the psyche, to which everything is related, by which everything is arranged, and which itself is a source of energy. The energy of the central point is manifested in the almost irresistible compulsion and urge to become what one is, *just as every organism is driven to assume the form that is characteristic of its nature, no matter what the circumstances. This center is not felt or thought of as the ego, but, if one may so express it, as the* self.

—Carl Gustav Jung

The moving point sweeps a line; the moving line sweeps a plane; the moving plane sweeps a solid.

—Euclid (ca. 300 B.C.)

The Pythagoreans divided the study of Number into four branches which may be analyzed in the following fashion:
    Arithmetic = number in itself
    Geometry = number in space
    Music = number in time
    Astronomy = number in space and time

—David Fideler

VII
Circumambulating

We tramped west across the island to the Bay at the Back of the Ocean and the Spouting Cave. The road was a straight ribbon west and took us past a few isolated crofts or small farms with lovely Gaelic names. We met a brown horse with a swishing tail and further on, an independently-minded black and white border collie. As we neared the Meadow of the Monks, the gulls began to show an expectant interest in us, and they circled lazily around us screaming and keening in what one must presume is "Gullic."

We talked again of Sophia and her function within us to guide and mediate between the outer and inner worlds. She has one end in view—to teach us that, despite the apparent dualities of existence, this world is a temporary illusion, a drama, a game that we have agreed to play while in the body. The real world is one and limitless, but for the sake of creation, manifestation, and consciousness, we have assumed it to be limited and obstructed.

You reminded me nervously of an incident in a class in Los Angeles, when I was sharing such a notion. As I was speaking the words, the blackboard suddenly fell off its easel straight onto my toes and broke one! We all laughed at the irruption of the Trickster, but I felt that I must complete the lecture as people had come from such distances.

During the break, I was enthroned in an armchair and my injured foot was placed in a bucket of ice water. Holding Woodstock for a pointer, I must have looked a mite odd. Finally, someone suggested that I looked like the caricature of a Tarot card. Och aweel! as the Scots say. I figured the lesson was that when incarnate, we have to remember this reality is not only three-dimensional but subject to weight and gravity. It was a painful reminder, but also funny.

I tried to reassure you, as I stopped to pull up a sock, that I had not forgotten the incident. Yet I could not help reciting Shakespeare to you. He said it best in the famous lines from *The Tempest*:

> Be cheerful, sir:
> Our revels now are ended. These our actors,
> As I foretold you, were all spirits and
> Are melted into air, into thin air:
> And, like the baseless fabric of this vision,
> The cloud-capp'd towers, the gorgeous palaces,
> The solemn temples, the great globe itself,
> Yea, all which it inherit, shall dissolve
> And, like this insubstantial pageant faded,
> Leave not a rack behind. We are such stuff
> As dreams are made on, and our little life
> Is rounded with a sleep.

By now we had reached the mysterious "golf course" on Iona. The only golfers I ever saw there were a few contemplative cows who contribute daily to the natural hazards of the course. But here the full breadth of the Atlantic Ocean comes into view, and the sounds of the waves sliding in with a strong swish and rippling up the inclines of white sand hits you as the echo is carried by the incessant wind. Today the waters were deep turquoise in the coves and clear and transparent over the rich assembly of stones that were gathered to the south—magical stones, luminous gems when bathed by the waves.

All the pleasures of the senses sweep through you as you breathe the salt air and look out to the sparkling expanse. The distant small islands were visible in the clarity of the day. As always in the Hebrides, they appear to float on a thin line of mist and seem disconnected from the vastness of the ocean. You have to catch your breath at the beauty of it all, and so we did.

We talked on, while we took off our boots and felt the cold, soft sand beneath our bare feet and between our toes. The good news, we agreed, is that the Holy Spirit (whose Age has come) dwells within us as the Paraclete—the Comforter, the Theotokos, the God-bearer, that process within each of us which can give us a "second birth" within the psyche, and which is always present in the sacrament of every minute. Despite her forced exile by Christian doctrine, she has persisted, in addition to the archetypal Fairy Godmother or the Guardian Angel beloved by children, in the teaching of the followers of hidden esoteric traditions in Europe. These devotees were willing to risk their lives as so-called heretics. (For a detailed account of Sophia's disguises, I recommend *Sophia: Goddess of Wisdom* by Caitlin Matthews.) For fear of their lives, the alchemists could only refer to Sophia as the "Dove" hidden in the "Stone," the Philosopher's Stone, that lies unrecognized on the common road of everyday.

"But why is it so difficult for some people to understand this?" you persisted.

"Mainly, I believe, because we have not kept the child alive in us, and we keep deflecting children away from the very gift they were born with. Remember that Jesus said that we could not enter the kingdom of heaven unless we became as little children. And he also said that the kingdom of heaven was spread all about us, but men could not see it. Sometimes there seems to be an enormous chasm between Christ and Christianity!"

"But how can we change this?"

I ventured that at the theological level, there is the movement begun by Matthew Fox called "Creation Centered Spirituality." Then there is the beautiful work of Teilhard de Chardin, and the current work of Brother David Steindl-Rast, and others, of course. At the psychological (and spiritual) level we have Jung and the many who have been inspired by him. It is he who made possible the idea that the Fall and Redemption of humanity are true for the ego. When we identify with the ego, we are out at the circumference looking for a God who is somewhere else—up there, out there like the sun in the sky. And since we live on the earth, this is only natural.

However, today we have a new icon—the picture of our Earth taken from the moon. Symbolically, this is very significant. The moon has made it possible for us to learn something outwardly that we could also learn inwardly—to get a new perspective on our own true nature. If we can hypothesize or have faith in the logic of the circle with its center, then we can more readily accept the inner presence of the Divine Guest, the Light Within us. "That's what is so significant about geometry. It is just so," I concluded.

"I never thought you could use geometry to prove the existence of God within us!" you laughed. "It boggles my mind."

"Well, you remember Descartes' *Cogito ergo sum*, I think therefore I am? That's the slogan of the ego. I had a dream once that said it should continue: *Ergo scivio Deus est*, therefore I *know* God is. It is a function of the ego to make creation conscious. The myth tells us that collectively we are to reclaim Sophia from her hiding place in so-called matter. It's called the 'anamnesis of Sophia.' Sounds like she has a cold or something, but it really means a recalling or re-membering of Sophia."

"So you do this by noticing things and events and connecting them to spiritual insights? Putting two and two together?" You stopped suddenly and stood looking out to sea. It was as if a great insight flushed your whole face. I waited to hear what it was. "*That means that synchronicity could be optional. You don't just have to wait around for it to happen!*"

"Phew! That's right. Usually we think of it as a serendipity, a coincidence that happens to us un-expectedly. 'An outer event that coincides with an inner meaning' is what Jung said it is. But every time you match the outer with the inner by searching for it, you might get an attack of insight, an Aha! You could get the hang of it and make it a habit!"

Instinctively, we sat down to ponder the tre-mendous implications of what had come to you. We spread out our jackets and sat looking out to sea.

I closed my eyes and felt the world briefly as one great

AUM

with the *AH* at the center, the *OOO* filling the circle, and the *MMM* brimming the edge and holding it softly together. I remembered seeing the picture in Hans Jenny's book *Cymatics* that showed that chanting the syllable AUM forms a perfect circle from small particles on a plate. They appear to be attempting to rise into a sphere. When we make that sound, do we surround ourselves briefly, I wondered, in a bubble of order and peace? It makes sense.

Sitting there, it was not too hard to extend my awareness to the great circle of the horizon, to feel the great throbbing circumference of space, to extend further out to the ordered panoply of heaven wherein we as one of the planets orbit the sun. With an immense extension of imagination, I marveled at anyone who could have discovered the zodiac, the great circle of constellations that mark the grand clock of Ages, which Hipparchus did two centuries before the Christian Era (the Age of Pisces). Circles, cycles, spirals—the ouroborus, the serpent swallowing its own tail. I remembered the beautiful drawing of Fludd's showing the Dove making a circular track in creation.

When I opened my eyes I could see the grass of the machain—that stretch of green that grows right down to the sea in the Hebrides—close beside me filled with tiny daisies and yellow flowers, each a small circle of perfection. I looked at you and thought gratefully that it had taken fifty-seven circular years for me to find you, but I did. And then I saw myself in Paris, when I was six, riding the little merry-go-round in the park, reaching and reaching for the brass ring. Then one day I caught it as we whirled by. What bliss! Decades later I exchanged this token for the wedding ring you slipped on my finger and the one I slipped on yours.

If we are each a circle, now it felt as if your circumference went through my center and mine through yours. And that is the symbol on the well at Glastonbury. It looks like this:

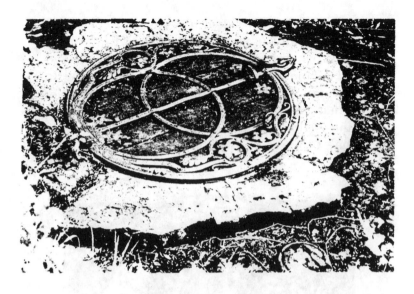

We continued to gaze out to sea. In the distance we could see the waves rushing into a cleft and shooting up high in the towering spume of Spouting Cave, like a geyser. Some seals were sunning themselves on the reef of a skerry. Gulls were waddling optimistically, not too near but not too far, as they saw a thermos and paper bags emerge from our knapsacks. It was time for a smackerel of something, as Winnie-the-Pooh would say.

Children dance Ring-around-a-rosy (the rose is a symbol for the Self); men and women in many countries do the same, and even Jesus spoke in the Gospel of John of the Round Dance. He said, "He who does not dance, mistakes the occasion." The Sufis dance in the round, as do the monks at Weston Priory, the Native Americans, and folk all over the world. Circumambulation is a holy act.

I remembered my struggle to ask the members of a class to stand in a circle and hold hands. It was the first time I taught at the C. G. Jung Foundation in New York. Forming a circle is a symbolic act and a way of reasserting that the true teacher is always invisible in our midst. You can hear that in two ways: in the circle itself or within each person. Ultimately, the only true guru is the Self, the Divine Guest. And the nice thing about a circle is that there's always room for one more.

We walked home in companionable silence. I could see that you were pondering something important. You took a shower and came out rubbing your hair dry and looking wonderfully tousled. Then you sat down on the edge of the bed and shot a question at me. "Why a compass and a straight edge? They, in themselves, must be highly symbolic."

"They are."

"The straight edge or right angle comes in handy for things like lines and squares and rectangles, and measuring fields and roads and practical things. It seems pretty masculine to me."

"What about the compass?"

"It makes wholes. It helps construct all the figures. It seems somehow feminine to me. Circles contain." You grinned at me. (I was a good example of circular amplitude.)

"The heavenly bodies all seem to be circular or spherical," you said, but you didn't mean mine.

"If your psyche has a centerpoint and mine has one, then we have two points." You reached for your copybook and made two points.

"This gives us a choice," you said.

"How?"

"Well, I can join them with a straight line using the straight edge, or I can choose one point and make a circle going through the other point. Like this.

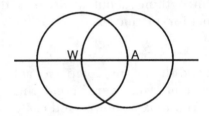

And if I call my point W and your point A, then you can do the same."

"That forms a *vesica piscis*," I said, and I shaded in the shape.

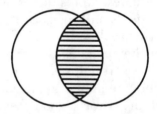

"The term actually means the bladder of a fish. It is the fish shape of the yoni and the symbol often used for Christianity, the great religious expression of the Age of Pisces, the constellation of the Fishes. In cathedrals you often find it containing the Virgin

Mary or Christ. It is a place for Sophia as well, since it is symbolic of the wisdom of feminine creativity. It is the fount of new birth itself.

"It seems like a sacred space for peace and harmony between people, when each person reaches out to embrace the Divine Guest or the center of the Self in another. Then the light multiplies."

"It's beautiful." You shook your head in wonder. I held my breath, waiting for what you would come up with next.

"I realize that when you use a compass you are adding a third dimension, both in fact and in consciousness. The point or pivot of the compass is the Third that makes Two, One. No, that sounds silly."

"It's not silly at all. It's profound. What you are saying is that duality or opposites themselves can be used to manifest a wholeness that is greater in content than what they started out with. The vesica piscis is the creative space, the yoni, where relationship can add something new. Two single circles can't do that. They have to 'coniunct!'"

"And if one goes through the center of the other, then it has to be radiant."

"What color would it be?" I mused.

"That's simple—the color of love," you laughed, snapping your book shut and giving me a teasing hug. "And now it's time for a little something." So saying, we dressed quickly and headed for the lounge.

Vocatus atque non vocatus Deus aderit.
Called or not called, God is present.
—The Delphic Oracle
(Words placed by Jung over his front door.)

The cross is the "I" crossed out.
—Sunday School Lesson (1931)

ABOU BEN ADHEM

Abou Ben Adhem (may his tribe increase!)
Awoke one night from a deep dream of peace,
And saw, within the moonlight in his room,
Making it rich, and like a lily in bloom,
An angel writing in a book of gold:—
And to the presence in the room he said,
　　'What writest thou?'—The vision rais'd its head,
And with a look of all sweet accord,
Answer'd, 'The names of those who love the Lord,'
　　'And is mine one?' said Abou. 'Nay, not so,'
Replied the angel. Abou spoke more low,
But cheerly still; and said, 'I pray thee, then,
Write me as one that loves his fellow men.'
　　The angel wrote, and vanish'd. The next night
It came again with a great wakening light,
And show'd the names whom love of God had blest,
And lo! Ben Adhem's name led all the rest.
—Leigh Hunt

Two is the first number because, with it, separation and
multiplication begin, which alone make counting possible.
With the appearance of the number two, another appears
alongside the one. . . . The "One" and the "Other" form an
opposition.
—C. G. Jung

On earth it takes two sticks to make fire.
—Mercy Muchmore

VIII
The Dividing Line

I t was early afternoon, and we decided to sit outside in front of the hotel on some white plastic chairs beside a round white plastic table. These were a source of amusement to us as they invariably blew over in the wind. But today was pleasant, and we could see the stretch of Mull across the Sound, "dreaming in sunlight" as the song goes. We had our books and implements with us and were ready to further our games with Sophia.

Our copybooks now had six entries: the blank page, the empty circle, the bindu, the circle with the center, the circle with the radius, and the two circles entwined.

I contemplated the straight line as the primal radius formed between the center and the circumference of the circle by the ego. Here, for me, was a profound proof of the duality the ego experiences through consciousness. This radius extends quickly into a diameter and the potential of many other radii.

According to Euclid, a line is the shortest distance between two points. It is length without breadth; it forms the first dimension by extension. This is a

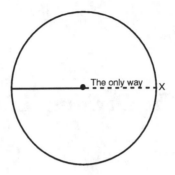

huge event! A line is capable of direction; the point can only hold position. With these thoughts in mind, we looked at a line solemnly, as if we had never seen one before.

A—————————————————————————B

We observed again that it seemed to imply division into two. A line had a beginning and an end, an above and a below. Already it suggested separation and otherness. Heaven is not earth, the horizon tells us. Man is not woman. "The line has been drawn in the sand," and what is mine is not yours. Oppositions are set up, and the sport has begun. Teams oppose one another and try to rush each other's goals. Wars are fought, and battle lines are drawn. It is ultimately a question of love or war, I or thou, the tug-of-war in this world and, above all, the primal sense of separation between us and God.

God, we are told, is all good, and we are a mixed bag, if not a hopeless case. This disturbed Jung a great deal, as we read in his "Answer to Job." Yahweh, according to the story in the Old Testament, seemed to have a shadow side, which Job protested against. This, for Jung, was a psychological turning point in evolution. Christ [consciousness] then came as a gift and a redemption.

Psychologically speaking, according to Jung, we develop an ego throughout our childhood. In the beginning, the infant lives in a sense of wholeness and undifferentiation (the ouroboric phase), and only slowly realizes that it is a separate being. As the mother of four children and grandmother of ten, I have noticed that this development usually begins with the word "mine!", with the infant's sense of possessing something. Prior to that realization, toddlers often refer to themselves in the third person. As the ego develops, so does consciousness, and ego-consciousness functions through duality. A "you" has appeared opposite to "me." Every parent has been through the terrible twos, when their sweet little angel suddenly discovers the power of "No!" against the parents' "Yes!"

In other words, all the divisions implied by that innocent looking line above hit us at once, as soon as we have been "cast out of Eden in our infancy," having eaten of the Tree of the Knowledge of Good and Evil and become conscious of opposites and capable of shame. Little Adams and Eves, we relive the reality, generation after generation.

To be conscious of anything at any given moment is to be thinking of this and not that. The brain has two hemispheres, and all but one of the intaking organs of perception—the eyes, the ears, the nostrils, the hands, and nervous systems—are dual. The exception is the tongue (when not forked!). All the senses report to consciousness, and the ego is the center of consciousness. It is through the ego that the Self is able to participate in life. The only problem is that we are apt to forget all about the Self, and think the ego is all that we are.

"Well, it makes life more dramatic," you said philosophically. "Wisdom surely consists in savoring life. The most interesting division for me is male and female, and as the French say, 'Vive la difference!' " You said this with such an engaging grin that I had to take a brief break in consciousness.

Anyway, you agreed that the ego comes up with the idea of I and not-I. This problem, you told me, occupied the German philosopher Johann Fichte a great portion of his life. It also interested Martin Buber, and he wrote his now famous work, *I and Thou* to point out that this relationship is more fruitful than I and it, where the thou is reduced to an object.

Our little straight line was drawing us into one of the most consuming dialectics of our time—the matter of *relationship*. Once the line is drawn, how do we get over it, under it, or do away with it? Today books and workshops offer advice to fathers/sons, fathers/daughters, mothers/daughters, mothers/sons, husbands/wives. Labor relations, national and international relations, our ecological relationship to the environment—we are all consciously involved in trying to solve these problems.

The most painful split, whether we like to admit it or not, is the sense of separation from the unity and wholeness we attribute to God. This drama of alienation is repeated in the microcosm of the human psyche in the separation of ego from Self. Once this break occurs, life eventually loses meaning.

It would seem, then, that once our little bindu, our centerpoint, has lost its innocence and extended itself into manifestation, we are forced willy-nilly to relate. It is here that Sophia waits for us. It is her gift and her comfort and her joy to teach us how to "unite" and reconcile these painful and yet necessary opposites. There can be no manifestation on any level without them. It is the line per se that brings us into the world of dimension and at the same time into relationship. Sophia, the wise and loving Comforter, waits on the bridge. As we reach out to cross it to the opposing side, she meets us halfway to guide us home. This lovely image appears in Persian literature where the figure of Daena, the embodiment of the soul's good deeds, waits to meet the dying one to guide him or her to the other side.

❖   ❖   ❖

I remembered that in *The Dove in the Stone*, I had written a bit about the impact of the horizontal time line of our lives:

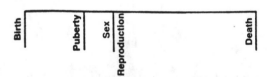

How devastating it is to think in terms of life and death as opposites, when, in truth, birth and death are really part of our greater life:

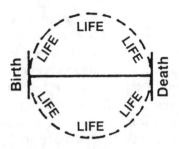

In sacred geometry, the horizontal line is considered feminine (not to be limited to female), and
in ancient Sumeria, the word for *plowing* and the
word for *coition* was the same. So the basic elements
of earth and water were seen to be yin or passive
and receptive, and the vertical line was seen to
be yang, masculine (not to be restricted to male),
as were the elements of fire and air. The sun's rays
fall from above, and so does rain. One of the Roman
god Jupiter's epithets was Pluvius, the Raining
One. So now we drew a vertical line:

C

D

We contemplated it. Our vertical line got us into the
dualities of left/right, high/low, up/down, powerful/
powerless, and the whole concept of hierarchies
and levels so dear to feudal or military patriarchal
thinking, and yet so organized:

God

Pope

Emperor

King

Prince

Duke

and so forth, down to the lowly serf or peon, each ideally the vassal of the one above.

We decided that we could make ladders and ladders of hierarchies in business corporations, in the military, in the Church, in government. There are even hierarchies of angels and archangels, and of devils and demons. Dante's Inferno is not unlike a department store of misery, nine floors to go down and others to go up to his Paradiso. In the East, you still see remnants of the caste system in India, and the great dynasties of ancient China had an equally rigid hierarchical system, though there it was determined not by birth but by merit and examination.

"Do we have such a hierarchy in the body?" you wondered. Then you answered your own question. "Of course, we do. It's the spine—thirty-three vertebrae and thus the thirty-three degrees in Masonry."

"Don't forget the chakras," I added. "They represent the hierarchy of consciousness."

You commented that the vertical ladder of power and ambition has caused as much suffering as has the horizontal one of despair. History is filled with stories of people struggling to reach the top and of

the wretchedness of those forced to remain at the bottom.

I pointed out that it is curious that humans are the only erect species. The paradox is that we sacrifice all rankings every time we fall asleep horizontally. In sleep, the king is no greater than the beggar.

"But this simple matter of walking upright and sleeping flat is too obvious. We don't connect it to one of Sophia's riddles," I said.

"Another curiosity is the fact that we have eyes only in the front of our bodies, and so we only can see an arc at a time, just as the circle of the rainbow shows only half of itself to our vision on earth. Consider the symbolism of the Pot o' Gold!

"We need a mirror to see our backs, and, in fact, we need mirrors to see all of ourselves reflected. All relationships involve reflections of each other. Each person we meet reflects another little piece of us that no one else can. That's another reason to love our enemy—he or she may reflect some dark part of us we do not wish to own. Many theologians of different persuasions maintain that God created the universe to see himself reflected."

We considered that there is yet another aspect to circles versus lines. Historically speaking, the oldest true democracy in the world is Iceland, founded in 936 A.D. Its parliament was called the Althing, and the members met out of doors in a circle. It seems a good sign that the Security Council of the United Nations also meets in a circular fashion. Most indigenous natives have always met in circles for councils and dances. By contrast, almost all churches,

theaters, classrooms, and lecture halls have been
set up in the dichotomy of preacher/congregation,
teacher/class, actors/audience, in twos, opposed to
one another. Only very recently has this begun to
change. We now have theater-in-the-round, and some
new churches are laid out in the round.

The exception all along has been the circus ring.
This ring has a strange etymological connection
to Circe, who lived on the isle of Aieia (five vowels!),
an isle of the dead. In ancient Greece funerary
games were held in her honor in a circle. These
games in a circle survived in the great amphitheaters
(a broken circle) in Greece and Ephesus and in the
circular Colosseum in Rome. Many temples and
domed cathedrals and chambers still have a circular
motif raised above a massive rectangular building.
St. Peter's in Rome, St. Paul's in London, and many
capitol buildings are good examples.

Returning to our two lines, we found that the next
move in the game was to intersect them. Of course,
there are myriads of ways of doing this, but only one
equal and balanced way. The result is a cross, one
of the oldest symbols in the world, and one of the
dominant symbols during the last two thousand years.

In sacred geometry, the cross is the symbol of
matter (with the masculine vertical intercepting the

horizontal feminine), as is its three-dimensional aspect the cube:

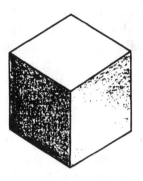

If we understand this, then the "crucifixion," symbolically understood, is true of all life that has incarnated into a world of duality, thereby experiencing the separation from spirit-as-unity. We have done a good job collectively in the last two thousand years of convincing ourselves that there can be no spirit in matter, a sure sign that we are identified with the ego. The task now is to see that this has been a dreadful fallacy. Matthew Fox's movement towards "Creation Centered Spirituality" is one of the most important steps being taken today to find that spirit has been hidden within this world of manifestation all along, only we have been too blind to see it. Sophia (Holy Wisdom) lies hidden in every atom and every stone, every tree and every flower. Her magic wand of revelation lies concealed within each of us.

When we came to the magic wand, you smiled. "Isn't that the meaning of the staff blossoming in *Tannhäuser*? Or the staff of St. Joseph of Arimathaea

that he planted at Glastonbury and which bloomed
on Christmas Day?"

"Or the words in the Twenty-third Psalm, 'Thy
rod and thy staff they comfort me.' Perhaps our spinal
shushumna in which kundalini rises is that very
staff." The wind began to rise, and you sneezed,
not once but about twelve times in succession, a
peculiarity of yours. I went in to get our sweaters.

After resettling, we looked at the cross on our page.

The powerful icon of the Age of Pisces is the
crucified Christ. Even for non-Christians, it is a
terrible spectacle—love rejected, love sacrificed.
But it is such a familiar icon that we fend off the
truth of it. It takes the eyes of children to make it
fresh once more. I know because when I showed
Giotto's picture of the crucifixion to one of my
daughters when she was four years old, she burst
into tears.

At any rate, we agreed that the cross is a profoundly
compelling archetypal paradigm set into history.
Yet, at another level, wherever we have a cross with
four 90-degree angles, we have an invisible circle
present, since the angles add up to 360 degrees.

"For me, I said, "this is a symbolic proof that there
is another world hidden in this one. And it's the
symbol of the Celtic cross. And it's the Celtic
Christians that never denied the sanctity of nature.
It adds up, doesn't it. Just look." I pointed to the
one we could crane our necks to see standing in
front of the abbey, St. Martin's Cross.

Furthermore, we could perceive, that wherever the vertical and horizontal intersect, a little "pook" of conception is possible. Psychologically speaking, that centerpoint or stillpoint is the center to yet another circle. An Aha! I drew again for review what we already had discussed—that if we sketch in the invisible circle (as in the Celtic cross) we create in terms of time a magical time out of time, synchronicity. It is acausal and always true of the psyche. It is "Once upon a time—" or what Jung called *illud tempus*, "that time." In terms of space, we have created a sacred precinct, a temenos.

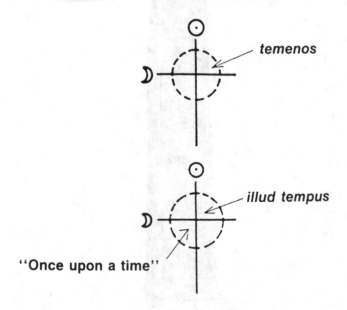

I added that for me, at any rate, it puts a whole new complexion on making the sign of the cross. We touch the Third Eye and draw a line down to the solar plexus, inviting the coniunctio to take place in the horizontal line that crosses our hearts. This is a true invocation, not so much a calling down, but a calling forth of the Divine Guest, the Light that is in us all.

Muslims make a similar gesture in the formal *Salaam* (peace), touching the three levels of consciousness: the heart, the mouth, and the forehead. The Hindus, instead of shaking hands, press their own two hands together (opposites) forming a closed circle of energy, and bow to each other saying *Namaste*, which means "I bow to the Divine in you." The sophistication of sacred symbolism in these two religions beggars belief. I believe such symbolism recurs because the practitioners all shared the same psychic or psychological insights.

"I've always been fascinated by hand gestures," you interrupted. "Can't they be symbolic, too?" Well, that set us off on an aside that fascinated us both.

"Oh, lovey," I cried, "that would have to be a whole other book. In India they are called *mudras*, and each one is shorthand for a whole message. Christian ritual and art have just as many. Have you ever noticed how popes and bishops hold their fingers? And think of how many ways we signal to each other with our hands instead of speaking. We have a whole silent language of signs." At this point I saluted you, wagged my forefinger, cocked a snoot, spiraled a finger to show how looney it all was, and laughed when you clapped.

This, in turn, led us to a discussion of *yantras* in India, which are purely geometric symbolic designs. Also, since by decree Islamic art must not involve depictions of people, the emphasis there has been even more on geometric design. It is not generally known that these designs have hidden teachings in them.

I drew an Indian yantra for Kali, the Mother Goddess of Hinduism:

"What do you think this might mean? Give just a gut reaction."

You looked at it. "It looks like a fancy bikini to me," you said sheepishly. But you had picked up the feminine symbol of the yoni immediately. Images are older and more powerful by far than words. "Remember that time you visited the ashram in Ganeshpuri? You said that every morning, a woman made a beautiful design with rice powder in front of the entrance? Wasn't that a yantra?" you asked.

I closed my eyes and vividly recalled the sight of the slender young woman in a red sari gracefully bent over the ground, sifting the white powder into the most exquisite and complex beauty, all done freehand. It was a mandala in honor of the god present in all who were to walk upon it. It just seemed a crime to set foot upon it, but you could not gain entrance without doing so. I remember standing there, listening to the birds calling in the garden, the heavy spring fragrance that is India, the bells chinking in the temple, and the endless chant rising and falling, over and over, "Hare Rama, Hare Krishna, Rama, Rama." The young woman artist spread her slender brown arms wide and with a flick of her hands offered the yantra to me, a first-comer. "Please," she encouraged, "please, it is for you." She meant the Divine Guest.

"Yes, that was a yantra, and it made me think in turn of the sand-paintings of Native Americans in the Southwest and those of the Buddhist monks making mandalas on the ground. They are all meant to be 'happenings,' temporary and spontaneously beautiful." I gave a deep sigh and ventured, "Most of us have lost the capacity to create and to sacrifice at the same time."

"Maybe that's exactly what divinity does," you added. "After all, you cannot sacrifice what you don't have, so by giving it away, you know for sure you had it in the first place."

"Huh? Say that again?"

"Well," you explained, "that's what makes it holy. *Sacri* means 'holy' and *fice* means 'makes.' That's how you get to keep what you give away. Remember those boys on the Ganges?" you went on, "they were making patties of cowdung, rolling them up into balls and slapping them on the wall to dry. But even doing that, they made a design, a yantra, and it certainly had the magic effect of a gift. I have never been able to forget it," you laughed.

I have given much thought to your remarks ever

since. It was the beauty and the power of the yantra that raised the simple act into something special. It ceased to be just cowdung or rice powder. I think of it whenever I see a bumper sticker complaining that "Life is just a ----!" Those Indian boys knew something we have yet to learn.

We mused that in the West, Pythagoras (ca. 600 B.C.) started the idea, it would seem, that geometry has some connection to the soul. He traveled to Egypt where, as we learn in the sixth grade, geometry began as a device to reclaim personal farmland after the annual inundations of the Nile. It began literally as "earth measurement." Circles were made with a peg and a rope. But our geometry texts often overlook the greatest geometric wonder of the ancient world, the Great Pyramid. Its base is thirteen acres! And there are no mistakes in its construction. I suspect Pythagoras was more interested in this kind of thing.

Plato, Euclid, Proclus, Nichomachus, and others continued the speculations and connections, but gradually a split took place, and the uses of geometry became profane. Its sacred aspect became one of the mysteries, taught and revealed only by secret initiation. To a certain extent this is still true. Sophia's role was hidden, but now we can look for her and find her, if we wish.

Today, geometry is almost exclusively a division of the study of mathematics taught for practical and technological application. In academia it has lost none of its powers but much of its soul. The Sophianic aspect of all of the sciences needs desperately to re-emerge. If it doesn't, we may well destroy our earth, and ourselves along with it. But should Sophia return to bring the soul back into the sciences, there could be hope. Jung prophesied that with the return of Sophia, a new age would begin.

The wind really picked up, and so we moved to a more sheltered bench in the hotel garden. It was under a sycamore tree with dark leathery leaves that rattled softly. The black rooks or ravens peculiar to Iona were calling one another.

"What you are saying is that, symbolically speaking, whenever we put the vertical and the horizontal together or try to bring spiritual meaning to something, we invoke Sophia."

"Yes, we invoke Sophia hidden in one of her drops of wisdom in our daily life whenever we connect 'an outward and visible sign with an inner and spiritual grace' of *meaning*. That's using the Christian definition of a sacrament for both synchronicity and the holy ground of a temenos. When invited, these can meet in any moment. It's our human privilege to live an examined life. You know—to see life, as that eight-year-old boy writing to Bronson Alcott in 1856 suggested, as 'the looking-glass of circumstance.' All life in this world is potentially holy, but we make a terrible mess of it through ignorance. I think it's consciousness and love together that can make any time in the world into magical time, 'once upon a time,' and any place into holy ground."

"But think of all the evil and horrors in the world," you protested. "They never seem to stop. People go right on killing each other, often just for the heck

of it. Don't take this personally: BANG, you're dead!
In the good old days people fought duels or punched
each other for reasons. Now they just shoot or drop
bombs as if it were all a video game." You shook
your head. "And almost all of the horror is caused
by humanity."

"True. But think of the cosmos. It has not ceased
to remind us of harmony and order. Nature teaches
us that there is destruction and darkness and pain
as well as beauty and calm. But Nature's destructive
aspects are not evil. We are. I really believe all evil
comes from ignorance and lack of balance. We are
always on the tightrope or what the Buddhists call
'the razor's edge.' That idea teaches that you have
to make your way *between* the opposites, neither
trying to be a goody-goody to get into heaven or
cynically denying the purpose to life and going to
hell in a bucket, as my mother used to put it."

"Aha!" you exclaimed. "A tightrope is another
line!"

"So it is. But just think of the *process* of relationship that it represents."

"In what way?"

"Well, the tightrope implies points A and B as the
posts, right? And you can't balance on a tightrope
or a razor's edge without reaching over the word
or to the word *and*. You teeter on the *ors* and fall
off, if you reject one side for the other entirely. So
you take a long pole to help you, which makes you a
living cross. That's another Mercy Muchmore!"

At that point, I got up and stretched out my arms
as I used to when I was a child and tried to balance
on an imaginary beam. Just then two proper English
ladies walked by on the other side of the garden

wall and smiled indulgently. They seemed to understand that you can do things on Iona that you wouldn't
think of doing elsewhere.

I stopped and closed my eyes. My arms were still
stretched out, and I had a flashing recollection of
cutting a string of paper dolls in a classroom in a
school in Italy. I thought I was cutting only one in
the folded paper, but out came six in a row. We
stuck the hands of the end dolls together with white
paste and they made a dance. A Round Dance. This
could mean not perceiving the cross only as the
crucifixion of the ego, but with the "I" crossed out
as extensions of hands and hearts to others in the
Round Dance that Christ spoke of in the Gospel
of John.

Jung wrote of this, as follows:

> The aim and effect of the solemn round dance [of
> Jesus and his disciples] is to impress upon the mind
> the image of the circle and the center and the relation
> of each point along the periphery. Psychologically
> this arrangement is equivalent to a mandala and is
> thus a symbol of the self.

I suddenly realized that all straight and divisive lines can be joined into circles when you lift them up into another dimension, because a circle is a two-dimensional figure and a line only one. It was a healing thought.

To juxtapose a little ring of flat paper dolls with Christ's Round Dance may seem strange, but I believe it would delight him. The dimensions of his dance were limitless, if you consider it, for it added not only a third, but a fourth. It was motion in time; it was love in motion; it was the planets dancing around the sun; it was the straight and divisive line joined through relationship into a circle of endless meaning. Were it not for twos, there could be no matter or love. So by dividing One, love was born.

As I stood there with my eyes squinched up, you got worried.

"What's the matter? Are you in pain?"

"No! I'm having an attack—"

"An attack of what?"

"Of insight, dear," I told you affectionately. I opened my eyes, and a rush of joy came over me. I tried to make sense of the images, and in the process I saw one more—the cross in M's room which always bore a fresh rose. It seems that it had taken forty years for that rose to open slowly in my heart. This very moment, on this holy isle.

We heard the dinner gong sound through the open windows. Time had flown by. We went in to wash up. As we sat down at our table, I noticed again our wooden napkin rings. They both bore the number 12. Your numbers were painted white and mine were painted black. We sat opposed to one another in love and merriment. The line WA extended to AO, from heart to heart. You poured the wine; I broke the bread and buttered it. We toasted each other in gratitude. And as we did, I knew that this, too, was a true communion. I was toasting the Divine Guest in you, who shines out so cheerfully through your eyes.

This night all the guests seemed special. The Chaplain to the Queen in his Aran sweater, the German mother and daughter, the reader of Camus, the young parents with the squeaky little ones wriggling on their chairs and banging their spoons on their plates, the Dutch hippie youth and maiden gazing passionately at one another and not tasting their food, and you and I. What can I say?

Later that night, when we went to bed, I found an envelope under my pillow. In it was a note that read:

Thank you for featuring us two straight lines. We have a problem relative. What do you suggest for:

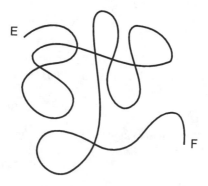

In great anticipation, love,

AB and CD

OPPOSITES: 1970

Always the supposition remains:
that the gagging ouroboros
the self-consuming fires
notwithstanding,
the tripod god
will keep us going after the Fall.

One black foot in heaven
one white foot in hell
a mind hot with love
a heart numbed by reason
we straddle and encounter
our dichotomies
spawning pain
inconsistencies and doubts.

Only at the outer limits
of our detumescent pride
do we sometimes remember
the Power of Three
and surrender humbly
starting without hope
centripetally
ineluctably called inward
perhaps to balance
and the One.

—A.O.

It is not what happens to a nation that counts, but how
it reacts to it.

—Arnold Toynbee

There is suffering in this world. All suffering comes from
attachment and desire.

—Gautama Buddha

Out of the One comes two; out of the two comes three;
and out of the three come the ten thousand things.

—The Tao Te Ching

IX
The Power of Three

The preceding poem "Opposites" was written years ago at a time of despair. It seemed to well up out of nowhere with a message of how to deal with painful oppositions in the psyche and in life. I remember lying on my bed and writing it, and shaking my head silently. I looked at the picture of the ouroboros on the cover of the book I was reading: a great feathered red and green serpent circled beneath the title with its tail in its mouth. I could remember only one other creature given to that activity—a crazy dachshund of a neighbor who would chase his tail in a frenzy until it collapsed in frustrated exhaustion. Without going into auto-biographical details, I confess that I was yet again at that place most of us arrive at one time or another. I was stuck. No hope, no way out. Somehow, evidently, I had read and remembered Jung's advice, "Hang on to the opposites!"

Recently, as I was riffling through a sheaf of old poems I had written, I showed you this one. You read it and looked up at me from your chair. "And who was the Tripod God? What was the Power of Three?" you asked.

127

"I honestly did not know at that time. I think I had to live it out in order to understand," I replied.

"How do you hang on to the opposites?"

"It's balancing pain with pain. It's living out a paradox by being as honest and detached about your feelings and your circumstances as you can be. It's trying to do what you feel is right in the face of what you think may be wrong. It's consciously choosing to suffer both alternatives simultaneously until the tension itself yields the solution. It's hanging on to duty and to desire, without denying either one."

I must have spoken with some passion, because you put your hand on my arm and said, "Then I understand. We were brought up to consider duty as the only choice. But sometimes it is our duty to ask why we have the desire and where might it lead. It might lead you to new growth. So often we feel we have to conform to something out there, and we conform ourselves right into the grave, proper to the end." You paused and added, "I, myself, used to be a terrible conformer. My mother was always concerned about what other people would think or say. It's like moral constipation. Nothing can happen."

"I'll say!" I laughed at your image. "But if you hang on to the opposites, sometimes fate takes pity. Something gives. As Jung says, if you change your consciousness, the outer events change of themselves. It's as if the outside is always mirroring our attitudes. There go all our favorite excuses, the 'if onlys.' I suppose we cannot always blame someone else; eventually we realize that unconsciously we have been colluding with our oppressor or the oppression."

"That's what Arnold Toynbee said about nations in history. It's not what happened but how they reacted. I suppose that explains how some people overcome poverty, sickness, and misfortune and end up the stronger for them, while others don't. I think of Beethoven at the end of his life, so deaf they had to turn him physically around to see the applause of the audience. He both accepted his handicap *and* proceeded to write the most beautiful music of his life."

"Or Brahms, so deeply in love with his best friend's wife, neither denying that love nor betraying his friend." We went on to share numerous examples from our own experience, none of them easy to bear.

We were sitting on the small beach near the jetty, just below one of the smallest post offices in the world, where we had mailed home some books bought at the abbey bookstore. The ferry had left and people had straggled away. The lady with the horse and buggy had delivered her tourists, and we could hear the clip-clop, clip-clop of the horse's hoofs going back up the road after the day's work. The water was calm, low tide, and some seagulls were wading peacefully in and out of the water. Two mongrel dogs were chasing each other, and a young mother sat in the sun watching her baby struggle to walk a few steps and then fall back on its diaper-padded bottom. This was a very determined little person.

I was pensive, realizing how you can wallow in blaming and self-pity for the rest of your days. During the so-called "consciousness movement" of the last few decades, an enormous amount of time and effort has been consumed in coming to terms with our unhappy childhoods, our terrible experiences of abuse, our inadequate parents, spouses, and on and on. It is important to confront these issues, but we can get trapped in this metaphor of blame and see no way out. Or we can use our scars as an excuse for all our failures. It really is true—our reality is always composed of the way we process experience. Like the baby so intent on walking, we need to get on with it in spite of the falls.

I watched the baby and the mother watching her child, thinking of my own children now grown and parents themselves, and I thought of all the youngsters I taught over the years. And I realized how great a debt I owe to Bronson Alcott, friend of Emerson, whose book *Conversations with Children on the Gospels* (printed in 1836) I had the good fortune to read as a young woman. Alcott was a teacher who truly believed the Divine Guest to be already present in every child. He knew that whenever that center in the soul (which he called the "imperial Self") remains unknown and unrespected in children, they have no point of referral within themselves or sense of self-worth. The same is true for the parents and teachers of such children. Then all relationships proceed ego to ego. The amazing thing is that those young pupils of his, five- to twelve-year-olds, had a clear understanding of what he was talking about. Though Alcott did not use today's terminology, in many of his observations and conclusions he anticipated Jung.

As we sifted sand through our fingers, we talked about three levels of love. We agreed that the first level is a child-like taking love, often full of need, attachment, and desire and fears of loss or rejection. This is how the ego begins the experience of love. Then it learns to exchange love with others, but there are still strings attached. It is as if two circles meet at the circumference. You sketched it out in the sand.

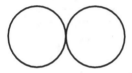

"It almost seems that if the ego is just a part of the psyche," you said, "it acts like a mirror. Like the moon that reflects the light of the sun, the ego reflects the light of the Self. Left to its own devices, the ego often feels dark and cold. So it reaches out.

"But, as I understand it, the Self needs the ego to distribute its love. Without this, it would burn up or consume those around, in the same way that probably nothing would unfold on this earth without the action of the moon, because it pulls the tides up in everything that grows. When, as it says in the *I Ching*, there is an attitude of devotion between the Creative [Self] and the Receptive [ego], then harmony prevails. We, ourselves, grow."

I chimed in. "Then the third level of love is out of and through the Self. It comes from a divine source. It has no need beyond giving. It just shines. Come to think of it, the sun never takes back its rays!"

"That is a fact!" you agreed firmly, and taking a stick you drew rays out of your circle in all directions.

One of the dogs came running to see what you were doing and was soon joined by the other. With their ears cocked high, they looked both comical and hopeful, wagging their tails and expecting you to come up with a bone. We petted them and threw the stick, and off they scampered. The baby's mother smiled. She got up, picked up her child, and carried him up to the stroller at the top of the beach. We, too, got up to go.

As we ambled slowly back to the hotel, my thoughts turned again to the Self. I believe that we are born sensing that we have that center. Every baby is a fresh start. It is virtually impossible not to be charmed by a baby. But what happens? All the worst criminals in the world were once lovable babies. Our educational system is not designed to keep alive that sense of the Divine Guest within. In fact, it contradicts that sense. No wonder the young are drawn to drugs— there is such an unconscious yearning in them. And not only in the young. William James called alcohol the cheap way to mysticism.

Apropos of this, I remembered an interesting conversation with my oldest grandson when he was four years old. His mother was in the hospital giving birth to his little sister, and he was in my care. Driving in the car, we passed a cemetery. My grandson said solemnly, "Gaga, that is a graveyard. They put you down there when you are dead."

"Is that so?" said I.

"But, you know what? Not the important part. The important part doesn't go down there."

I was duly impressed, so I ventured to ask, "Where was your important part before you were born?"

There was a long silence, while I drove around several curves in the road. I stole a look at him as he struggled with the question. Finally, he turned to me, wide-eyed in consternation. "Oh!" he cried out, "I forgot! I forgot!" But he knew that he had known. I believe this is true of all of us.

My mind then went to the exercise in identity I sometimes give my adult students. It goes like this:

Close your eyes. Think back to the earliest memory you have of being you. Why was it important to know that you were you? When did you begin to have opinions of your own about people and about life? When did you first ask Who am I? Why am I? Or do you have, like so many others, very little recollection of your childhood? The first questioner in the psyche is, of course, the budding ego. But all along, love, as an irresistible force, has its origin elsewhere than the personal ego. The ego personality that we give our name to truly only reflects and transmits it.

Someone may write and I may read, but I will not be reading precisely what the author wrote. I will be reading that which is meaningful to me. All the while, each of us is reading a different book. A good poem makes a poet of the reader. When I read something that rings true and goes straight to my heart, or hear or see it, that Aha! feeling comes. I know that I am in the presence of something greater than I am. The Self of that other has touched mine and stirred it to life.

I believe that we really can never claim creativity. We can only submit to it since we ourselves are created. Those who see themselves as creators open themselves wide to inflation and narcissism, often an occupational disease that artists succumb to. It really pays to remember that it is only the Sophia in each of us who can write the "lively word," the word that quickens. It reminded me of words of D. H. Lawrence, who said, "As we live, we are transmitters of life." I could only remember a fragment of a poem that he wrote:

> Give, and it shall be given unto you
> is still the truth about life.
> But giving life is not so easy.
> It doesn't mean handing it out to some mean fool, or
>   letting the living dead eat you up.
> It means kindling the life quality where it was not,
> Even if it's only in the whiteness of a washed pocket-
> handkerchief.

I mused that this hunger to know, to experience the Source, is to the ego what geotropism is to any seed. I wondered if you, too, had planted a bean upside down (on purpose) in a paper cup in first grade. I put mine on the windowsill, watered it, and watched for what seemed centuries for something to happen. Then suddenly it did. The lesson is that, upside down or not, the bean grows up, reaching for the sun. Years later, I realized that I have an upside-down ego, or else it would not have taken so long for me to accept on faith and logic the obvious lesson of the circle which teaches the same process. So that inner reaching to the glowing center from the circumference has to be "the Only Way."

In fact, the great Teachers all tell us about the Light that we are seeking. Were we to find it, we would be more "enlightened" or more "illuminated." Not a single one of them boasted, anymore than a flower does. They just shone, and the Sun behind the sun shone *through* them. I imagined how the lovely words of Thomas Moore could be applied to the soul:

> No, the heart that has truly loved never forgets
> But as truly loves on to the close,
> As the sunflower turns to her god when he sets
> The same look which she turned when he rose!

As we rambled back to the hotel, people overtook us as they walked energetically, bent up the hill towards the abbey. Others walked down past us, most of them giving a quick, friendly nod. Occasionally someone would stare self-consciously ahead, either too shy or too introverted to connect. We turned in at the gate to the hotel and went to our room for our copybooks, and ended up having tea in a corner of the lounge.

We pictured the ego hanging onto the opposites for dear life, which means choosing "and" instead of "or." Geometrically, we still had our lines and the cross of duality. We remembered the "pook" of the coniunctio where the two lines intersected. We also saw that in the process of determining a vertical line to intersect the horizontal one, we had to make little arcs to locate the points. The top point made it possible to make the first enclosed figure of geometry using straight lines—the triangle. With that we had advanced to another—the second dimension. A big step! The triangle, using only three lines, is the first enclosed space possible.

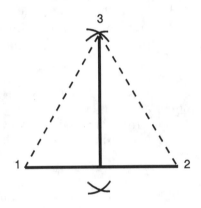

So in progressing from 1 (point) and extending it into 2 (line), we now had 1 + 2 = 3. It seems almost a joke that the sign for "plus" is a cross.

"What could be the psychological interpretation of this simple construction?" you wondered. I replied that Jung had a term for it—the transcendent function. He wrote:

There is nothing mysterious or metaphysical about the term "transcendent function." It means a psychological function comparable in its way to a mathematical function of the same name, which is a function of real and imaginary numbers. The psychological "transcendent function" arises from the union of conscious and unconscious contents. . . .

The shuttling to and fro of arguments and affects represents the transcendent function of opposites. The confrontation of the two positions generates a tension charged with energy and creates a living, third thing—not a logical stillbirth in accordance with the principle *tertium non datur* but a movement out of the suspension between opposites, a living birth that leads to a new level of being, a new situation. The transcendent function manifests itself as a quality of conjoined opposites.

In other words, out of the tension of the opposites, a solution is found by looking at the problem from another level or dimension. In a film interview, Jung contrasted himself with Freud, as Jung had always been a student of Hegel's philosophy. It was Wilhelm Friedrich Hegel who called the opposites *thesis* and *antithesis* and reconciled them in *synthesis*. Jung then gave this concept a psychological application. It seems almost as if the conscious provides the thesis and the unconscious the antithesis, and that if we hang onto and yoke the two, the result could be a synthesis.

It is very wise to ask for help from the unconscious. Jung recognized this process as central in alchemy. This is shown in the many symbols of coniunctio or union of the King and the Queen, the Sun and the Moon, the gold and the silver. In fact, Jung's last major work was entitled *Mysterium Coniunctionis*, the mystery of the conjunction of opposites, or the *coincidentia oppositorum*.

To this you added, "Papa, Mama, and baby make three." Then you hastily apologized for bringing the conversation down to such a level.

"I'm sure Jung would have loved the remark—it only proves the point!"

"I am beginning to realize," you summarized, "that if the time the Self lives in is synchronicity, and the place is the *unus mundus* or that world hidden within this one, and the loving eye of the Self is the Third Eye, then for Jung, at least, the Self speaks Latin! Every time he has something really important to say, he lapses into Latin."

"That certainly seems true. Perhaps it's his way of marking something special. Latin and Greek and Sanskrit and Hebrew and Arabic are all said to be sacred languages."

"In what way?"

"Simply because of the purity of the vowels used. Some people have pointed out that vowels correspond to the chakras, and when they are chanted, they affect us physically and can affect our consciousness. During the Renaissance, they added another element —music was even composed to fit the geometric architectural space within a church in Milan. This was purposefully done to lift the consciousness of the people hearing it. It may sound far-fetched, but when the Roman Catholic church abandoned the mass in Latin, something in that direction was lost. In fact, a study of some monks in a monastery was done recently. They decided to cut back on Gregorian chant to save time. The result was a noticeable drop in the monks' energy. Now some musicologists are recovering this information. Music can have a powerful effect on the psyche for good or for bad.

Sometimes it leads you where you would not go."

"That's very true," you said seriously. "I think we should add that music can be the language of the Self. When it is beautiful, it can heal the soul and bathe it with hope." You reminded me of our recent visit to Russia and how, despite all the hardships and lack of food, you could turn from station to station on the radio and hear the most glorious classical music. There was even a concert in Moscow in honor of Sophia.

As we continued our work, we found a number of intriguing things about triangles. First, the angles of *any* triangle always add up to 180 degrees or half the degrees of a circle.

"To me, this suggests a need for two triangles to get together," you said. "Then they would add up to 360 degrees. If the feminine triangle is the bikini, then the masculine one is upright. You put them together and you get this, a hexagram":

This symbol, often called the Star of David, follows the pentagram, also known as the Seal of Solomon.

As important as the Mogen David, the symbol of Judaism (it is on the flag of Israel), both symbols are universal. And, indeed, the interlaced triangles are symbolic of the union of masculine and feminine. In India, the figure is known as one of the yantras, the name given to diagrams helpful to study and meditation. The most complex one of all the yantras is called the Sri Yantra (the Lord of Yantras), and it is said that you can get lost trying to count the number of triangles in it.

We tried counting them for a while and gave up. Then we discovered that if you draw a triangle in half a circle, it will always be a right-angled triangle with the diameter of the circle forming the hypotenuse. Shades of Pythagoras!

Of course, there are many different kinds of triangles. But, as you pointed out, the Power of Three and the transcendent function suggest the

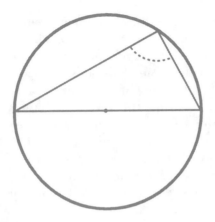

triangle formed by the tightrope walker's head and his hands on the pole, or the weighing scales of a balance—the equilateral triangle. You drew one:

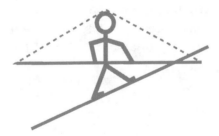

We noticed that in Christianity, this triangle symbolizes the Holy Trinity: God the Father, God the Son, and God the Holy Spirit or Hagia Sophia. For some early Christians, Sophia was seen almost as God's anima.

Here in our village, a neighbor's little girl recently asked her parents if Mother Nature was God's wife. Such ideas, it seems, have a life of their own.

Now, we needed a triangular compass of two legs to draw a circle. So psychologically speaking, the Self needs the ego and its comforting guide (Sophia) to become Self-conscious or conscious of the Self or Divine Guest within, and thus become capable of creating the circle of totality. So symbolically the triangle becomes the active agent in the process of the transcendent function. In a way, it describes the very process of individuation. It forms the model by which we and all life grow out into multiplicity. As the Tao Te Ching says:

> Out of the One comes the two; out of the two comes the three; and out of the three come the ten thousand things.

I speculated further. The triangle also demonstrates how we grow inwardly by "putting two and two together" with the help of our inner trinities. The ego experiences the opposites. Sophia or our intuition mediates between the ego's opposites and lifts them

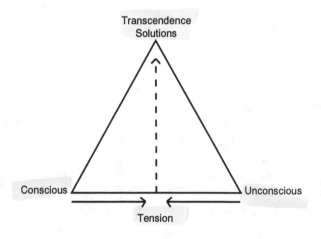

toward the Self by extracting spiritual insight from experience. To the degree that we achieve this, we grow in wisdom.

Moreover, and most significant, when we apply Sophia's game of matching the outer event with spiritual implication, we generate an *active* synchronicity. Normally, we experience synchronicities passively and just wait for them to occur. But with a certain attitude towards them, they can happen with greater and greater frequency, because we ourselves supply the meaning. We had agreed that synchronicity is the time in which the Self lives. Perhaps it works like this: We have an Aha! A perpendicular shoots up out of the tension of the line to form a triangle, just as surely as a sprout shoots up from the two halves of its bean.

I digressed here to remind you of just such a synchronicity that we once shared. I was giving a workshop in Bath, England, in the famous Pump Rooms, and you were there, too. Present in the group was an elderly man who had lived all of his life in Bath and from childhood had sung in the cathedral choir. We discussed Jung and synchronicity, and I shared the idea of the Ahas! in life.

During the lunch break, this man wanted to show us the cathedral, which was on the same square as the Roman baths. No sooner had we entered the beautiful dark, hushed atmosphere of the church than we looked up at the great perpendicular stained glass window which dominated the wall behind the raised altar. Breaking the silence, you pointed with a great gasp of delight to the top of this window and cried, "AHA!" Sure enough, the stone arches formed, clear as clear, the letters A H A. Our choir singer clapped his head in amazement. "But I've sung here for over sixty years and never ever saw it!" He was delighted and thoroughly convinced of synchronicity.

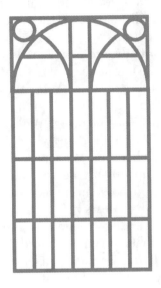

We reminisced about this, and then you interrupted the conversation to hottle up the tea in your cup from the samovar. When you returned and sat down, you put into words a question I had been asking myself for some time. "Why is it so important for us to express these things geometrically? Why not just leave them in words?"

"That's a good question," I said. I told you what I learned from M starting me in this direction is that mathematics and geometry provide us with irrefutable proof of certain basic things. They function at the level of "just so." You can see in a flash, as did the ancient Greeks and great mathematicians of old, that certain things—perhaps very few—are true: $1 \times 1 = 1$, and $1/1 = 1$. Multiplying and dividing, one remains one. But $1 + 1 = 2$, and $1 - 1 = 0$. Adding and subtracting, one changes one. The mystics read wisdom into this, and so can we.

As Proclus says, we have these figures built in. We project upon them, and then with guidance, we rediscover them.

For me, it is one of those places where science and religion could meet. Philosophers play mental games of semantics with Sophia, but geometry is even more profound. It is something we can actually see and experience, not just speculate about. So we can "prove" Jung's concept of the transcendent function geometrically. It works in the pure abstract, but it also works in life, both in the outer world of nature and in the inner world of the psyche. I find that very comforting. It is Sophia's way of showing forth—her epiphany, as it were. When we appeal to the unconscious sincerely, something usually comes to us "out of the blue"—and, oddly enough, that is the color attributed to her.

I paused, hunting for words, because it meant so much to me to say it right. "We are told again and again that nothing is hidden. It is all there, but we are blind or not taught where to look or how to see. Sophia cannot hit you over the head with her magic wand but, as Mercy Muchmore tells me, you have to be humble enough to study the obvious. As the alchemists said, we walk over the philosopher's stone everyday without knowing it."

You were bent over your copybook, and I could easily imagine you as a boy many years ago, wearing that earnest look, a lock of unruly hair over your forehead. The light fell upon our teacups, the circles of our little plates, and across your big polar bear paws carefully holding the slender compass. How could one not look upon you with a loving eye!

You caught my glance. "What are you thinking?" you asked mischievously.

I looked up at the ceiling. "The perfect hexagram!"

Only subjective [ego] consciousness is isolated; when it relates to its centre it is integrated into wholeness . . . if you can see and understand your suffering without being subjectively involved, then, because of your altered standpoint, you also understand "how not to suffer."

—C. G. Jung

Out of the Third comes the Fourth as the One.

—Axiom of Maria Prophetissa the Alchemist

Hidden in the Fourth is the One. Find him by uniting the Two in the Third.

—A.O.H.

Find the only Who in the What. Here is How!

—Mercy Muchmore

In relation to the special conditions of our world . . . the limits of quality and quantity are an expression of the two universal principles which elsewhere have been referred to as "Essence" and "Substance," and they are the two poles between which all manifestation is produced.

—René Guenon

I didn't come to create any problems
I'm only here to love.
A Heart makes a good home for the Friend.
I've come to build some hearts,
I'm a little drunk from this Friendship—
Any lover would know the shape I'm in.
I've come to exchange my twoness,
to disappear in One.
He is my teacher, I am His servant.
I am a nightingale in his garden.
I've come to the Teacher's garden
to be happy and die singing . . .

—Yunus Emre (14th century Turkish Sufi poet)

X

Qualities and Quantities

ur next adventure on Iona was another excursion to the so-called Hermit's Cell, a ring of stones which might or might not be the ruins of a cell of Columba's—in any case a magical spot to meditate and look out west to the Atlantic.

This day, the lateness in the season notwithstanding, was the hottest day we had ever encountered on the island. It might have been close to 80 degrees, almost unheard of. In Scotland you read of the temperature "soaring into the seventies!"

We set off too early to anticipate what was to come, but as we crossed the long "vallium," the grass-covered wall surrounding the now vanished ancient monastery, we began shedding our jackets and sweaters, packing them away in our rucksacks. The sun was oppressive; there was no breeze, just a mass of hot and hazy air. Nevertheless, we climbed on, up and down, over hills and heather-covered hummocks, through bogs and bracken. Because of the heat and still air, the fragrance of the earth was pungent and sweet, especially the heather.

There is not a spot on Iona without a name. We

149

crossed the Meadow of the Lapwings, looking ahead for the Hill of the Querns, which broods over the Well of the North Wind. For us at our age, it was fairly strenuous going. At one point we had to wriggle flat on our stomachs under a stretch of wired fence. This involved one of us passing all our gear over the fence to the first successful wriggler, and we ended up soaked and cooled by the bog, which on this day felt good.

We finally rounded the big hill called Cnoc nam Bradhan Mhor and, to our delight, saw the ring of stones. Each year, each time, I find myself praying to be able to see it one more time. There was not a soul around. The heavy, still, hazy air hung suspended, and a mist stretched wide out to sea.

We had just managed to get to the stones and to fish for our picnic in our rucksacks when the attack came. Out of nowhere, a huge cloud of Scottish midges descended upon us and every conceivable bare spot of our skin. These midges are notorious, but you really have to experience them firsthand to appreciate how awful they are. They bite and sting like tiny needles; they get into your nose and ears and up your sleeves and down your neck and back, and sting and sting and sting. Desperately, we tried to cover ourselves. I was lucky, because I had a hood on my poncho, but you were being devoured. I never saw you walk so fast. All one could do was splutter. I would have cried out my sympathy except that to open one's mouth was an invitation for a few thousand midges to drop in for lunch. It certainly taught me why Beelzebub, the demon, is called the Lord of the Flies. It took several weeks for those bites to disappear from our faces and arms, and the itch remained as long. Fortunately, midges only like warm, motionless air, usually a rarity on that windy isle.

We took refuge in the Abbey Coffee Shop and cooled off with cold sparkling apple juice. As I let the cool liquid slide down my throat, the thought shot through that it is the *quality* of an experience that remains with us long after the experience itself. This must be what the Divine Guest gathers up and carries softly away from the quantity of our passing days. It is the elixir that we carry with us, perhaps even after death. I know that I was hot and blotched with bites, but what I remember is the cool sparkle, the healing sweet of that draught of relief. I still taste it.

Needless to say, at this point, our geometric philosophizing was limited. It was only much later that the idea of not having to take all this into the circle of our souls recurred.

I tried to remind myself how tempting it is to get mad or become irritated when things turn out quite differently from what we expect. Yet we always have the chance to make that a conscious choice. When we get angry or resentful or irritated (and who doesn't), it usually means that we are "hooked" unconsciously or have a gap in the circumference of our circle that signals a need to deal with something. Life is full of unexpected events.

This one with the midges, however, was not worth taking into one's soul, so I tried to see the comic side of it. Over the sips of cider, I reflected that it is even harder to apply conscious detachment to personal relationships than to external events. And yet I had just witnessed a mother in Oban confronted by her frustrated little boy stamping his foot and crying out, "I hate you! I hate you!" She was smiling at him and trying to wipe away his tears with her hanky. You could see that she was thinking how cute he looked when he was mad. Her love protected her completely from taking his words personally.

This kind of detachment gets much harder between grownups, and the problem magnifies with groups. But when you think of Jesus' words, "Forgive them, they know not what they do," the process of great compassion is revealed. One of the signs of a true Teacher is that the Teacher does not take insult or rejection personally. Again, it is love that prevents this from happening. Even the anger Jesus displayed at the moneychangers in the temple was *ad rem* and not *ad hominem*. It is a very tall order, but it is surprising how often we are tested in this area. I realize now that I never saw M angry.

It was M, in fact, who told me of the distinction between those Latin expressions. "They are legal terms," he said, "but they come in mighty handy by distinguishing your attitude towards people. When you argue *ad rem*, you are discussing the matter at hand, the issue itself. You can protest it or argue for something better. When, on the other hand, you argue *ad hominem*, that means you are attacking your opponent personally and emotionally. You see that all the time in politics, but it can happen in families just as often." He then pointed out to me that in dealing with my own small children, it was always wiser to say, "That's a no!" than to accuse the child of being naughty. It directed the child's attention to the matter in question rather than making it feel guilty. It was very wise advice. He also had this to say, which made me think of the balancing of opposites. "If a child is running and bangs its head on the corner of the table and starts to cry, direct its attention to the table. Is it broken? Is it hurt? Poor table! This will distract the child from its own pain and train it to be sensitive to the other, whatever or whoever that might be." I have seen mothers do just the opposite and encourage their children to attack the object instead and project blame upon it. It may seem a small matter, but it forms a habit of taking more conscious responsibility at an early age.

These thoughts reminded me of the young Krishnamurti's advice always to give in graciously in matters of no consequence, but never in matters of principle. However, those midges . . . ! I looked at you and saw you rubbing your arms ruefully but smiling, as well. I relaxed. The day had not been a total failure.

Later when you were splashing around, cooling off in the tub, we got back to triangles. The subject of the anima and the animus came up.

"Jung named the anima the inner feminine side of a man, and the animus the inner masculine side of a woman, am I right?" you asked.

"Yes, that's right," I replied.

"Well, how did he discover them?" you asked.

It so happened that I had recently read that story in a book by Marie-Louise von Franz. It sheds light on how frequently in his life, Jung would examine an event objectively when it occurred. He practiced this all of his life. It was not enough just to accept things; Jung always pushed on farther, asking why.

I told you that at one time, according to von Franz, Jung had a woman patient of great charm and beauty. He confessed that he was much taken with her. However, during the analysis, this woman apparently lied to Jung more than once. He was greatly shocked. He could never have believed such a thing possible. He felt hurt and betrayed by this lovely lady. Then he reflected about it and began to ask himself *why* he had such high expectations of this woman. He concluded that he had projected his own ideal of the feminine upon her, almost as an inner vision of his own soul. Upon further reflection, he saw this as something all boys and men are wont to do, including many of his patients. They fall in love with their own projected goddess—their soul, their anima. On further reflection he realized that girls and women do the very same thing with their ideal of the masculine, and so for them, he coined the word *animus*.

I shared this tale with you, sitting at the end of the bed and talking through the bathroom door. When you raised your poor arms to soap them, I could see the many midge bites.

"That makes a lot of sense, doesn't it," you said. "It explains all the heartaches that we have when we are looking for our true love. So often she doesn't fit the image we have of her inside. But think what would have happened to Dante if he had married Beatrice and had twelve little round Italian babies!"

"The same is true for women, dear," I responded with a deep and knowing sigh. "We, too, keep putting our ideal image like a veil in front of one man after another, and most men can't take that, let alone boys." I was thinking of my first great passion for a boy in the sixth grade, and quite a few more farther on.

"But Beatrice led Dante to paradise, so the anima must have a good purpose, painful or not."

"Well, according to Jung, her purpose is to lead a man eventually from the personal unconscious to the collective—to the kingdom of heaven within, where the Self dwells."

"That makes two more triangles, doesn't it? Goodness, that makes a double wedding for us—you and me, my anima and your animus."

"Double the pleasure, double the fun!" I retorted.

There was more splashing from the tub, and I knew you were getting out and wrapping yourself in a towel. Sure enough, you entered into the room in stately fashion, looking like Jupiter in a toga. I decided that perhaps my animus had grown up a bit since the sixth grade. I really liked what I saw.

You stood there still dripping and said, "You know, that really makes a lot of sense. I think I had a wonderful anima dream just the other day, but it wasn't about you." You looked apologetic and sheepish, but I assured you animas are always personal to each individual. I was just happy that it was a good dream. I had no idea that it would be a classic!

You sat down beside me, and here is the dream you told me:

> I dreamt that I was at a beach, which formed a large half-circle, somehow like a waxing moon, and I stood at the lower end of it. A city was in the far distance. The beach was crowded with many people sunbathing, playing, and swimming. The bay was actually an inlet from the ocean, which was to my left, but it was separated from the ocean by a huge black curtain which stretched across the entire mouth of the bay.
>
> I was with a young woman, whose face I do not

remember. However, I did know that she was beautiful. We decided to swim naked to the ocean. In order not to create too much attention, we quickly undressed, jumped into the bay, and swam out to the curtain. Quickly we ducked under it and swam out to the ocean, which was pleasantly cool. I swam on my back, and the young woman floated right above me. Our skins touched and caused a blissful feeling.

Then we returned, swimming again underneath the curtain and back to our spot to dress again. Immediately, a tall man—a foot taller than I—appeared and accused us of indecent behavior and called the woman a whore, whereupon I knocked that man down with one blow of my right fist. I was amazed that I was strong enough to do that.

I pointed out that the unconscious often appears as water in a dream. Your anima seemed to have led you past the dark curtain of the personal into the greater waters of the collective unconscious. The blissful floating there together is depicted oddly enough in many alchemical drawings. The end of the dream revealed that you overcame your shadow, the man who was reproaching you for not conforming to convention. It truly was a great dream.

Of course, there are many variations on the theme of the anima. She can appear to men as a witch, a bitch, a seductress. For Dante, she was Beatrice and for Novalis, his beloved Sophie. In both cases, as with Yeats as well, real women became *femmes inspiratrices*, inspiring the creative impulse towards soaring heights of beauty. Here the anima and the muses interweave. It occurred to me again that works which become classics touch the archetypal realm, and so they become meaningful throughout time. The rest remain period pieces.

I tried to sum up what the day and you had taught me. It is that love solves those painful opposites, both within and without. The love that men and women have for each other, which can be so full of pain as well as of joy, is an outer event helping us to eventually consummate the oppositions within us. We usually begin by losing ourselves in each other, until Sophia comes along to remind us that personal love eventually leads to transpersonal love. Thus the addition of the third point of the spirit sanctifies relationship. This is beautifully portrayed in an alchemical drawing of the union of the King and the Queen.

It is a hint that wherever there is true love, Sophia is hidden in it. The same message is hidden in the Tarot card called "The Lovers." There an angel hovers over the two making the third.

In most myths, the gods do not display themselves full-blown to mortals. Even Zeus, who had a seemingly endless penchant for mortal women, was tactful enough to assume disguises, now as a bull, now as a swan, now as a shower of gold. In the Old Testament, we are told that no man can see God and live. But there is at least one exception in Greek mythology. It is the myth of Philemon and Baucis. Oddly enough, this was my favorite myth when I was a child, and my grandmother read it to me out of Hawthorne's *Tanglewood Tales*. Briefly the myth goes as follows and I whispered it to you as we lay in bed that night.

> Once upon a time, the world was in such a terrible state, and people were so wicked, that Zeus decided to destroy it. He shared this idea with Hermes, his messenger, but Hermes suggested to Zeus that they might both disguise themselves and check things out one last time.
>
> Without further ado, they dressed as tramps and descended to a village. Here they knocked on doors and begged for a little food to sustain them, but at every door, they were met with rude rejection. "Be off, you beggars! Off, off!"
>
> Zeus was getting mad. "That's it!" he cried. But Hermes pointed out a little hut off by itself up the hill. "Just one more chance!" he pleaded.
>
> Now it so happened that an old couple called Philemon and Baucis lived in that hut, and they were the poorest villagers of all. Nevertheless, when the tramps arrived, they were immediately invited in, dusted off, and clucked over by Baucis, and made to

sit down and rest by the compassionate Philemon. Next, husband and wife went to get them some milk, but to their dismay, they found that they had hardly any at all. Nevertheless, two cups were brought in, and Baucis poured all that she had into the cup for Zeus. As she poured, the milk kept flowing out of her jug until not only his cup but that of Hermes was filled as well.

By now, the husband and wife were aware that something miraculous was occurring. Anxiously they looked at each other and at their scruffy guests, whereupon Zeus stood up in all his glory, and Hermes likewise, and the two gods revealed themselves to the two poor peasants. Not only that, but because of their love for one another and their kindness and generosity to passing strangers, Zeus told the couple that if they had one wish, he would grant it.

After the two old people consulted one another, they faced the gods and humbly confessed that since they loved one another so much, they really had only one wish—not to be separated after death. And their wish was granted. When they died, Philemon became an oak tree and Baucis a willow, and to this very day their branches intermingle.

I can honestly say that this is still one of my favorite myths, and I knew that you would pour out your last swallow of milk with as whole a heart, as Philemon and Baucis did. Some things never change.

In literature triangles frequently mean love triangles. In fact, that would be most people's first association with the word. But if the One produces the Two, then the secret of any triangle lies with the Third from the point of view of the Two—that point in which any Two always remain One (Spirit). This is a paradox, a koan. Each of the Two is actually a One:

1

1   1

One is both a quantity and a quality. *Perhaps it takes the Two to make the quality of that initial quantity conscious.*

How gently, gently Sophia was leading my thoughts. She was constantly beckoning me to notice that hidden quality in all things.

That night when we were almost asleep I tried touching your left hand with my left and your right hand with my right. Were we to dance that way, our arms would make a leminiscate, the symbol for eternity. And since for us here in this dimension, eternity is in the moment "now" (the point in time), maybe Iona is a point in space where we were living more in quality than quantity. I tried feeling the quality of the sheets, the quality of the open window framing the silver sea, the quality of the soft Hebridean night, the dear quality of your shoulder barely yet sturdily visible. I realized that for me this was the secret of these shapes we were studying—all of them—they led me straight and safely from the measurable of all externals to the immeasurable of appreciation, experience, and love.

I swear by the discoverer of the Tetractys, which is the spring of all our wisdom, the perennial fount and root of all Nature.

—The Pythagorean Oath

Straight, square, great, without purpose, yet nothing remains unfurthered. The symbol of heaven is the circle, and that of earth is the square. Thus squareness is a primary quality of the earth. On the other hand, movement in a straight line, as well as magnitude, is a primary quality of the Creative. But all square things have their origin in a straight line and in turn form solid bodies. In mathematics, when we discriminate between lines, planes, and solids, we find that rectangular planes result from straight lines, and cubic magnitudes from rectangular planes. The Receptive accommodates itself to the qualities of the Creative and makes them its own. Thus a square develops out of a straight line, and a cube out of a square. This is compliance with the laws of the Creative; nothing is taken away, nothing added. Therefore the Receptive has no need of a special purpose of its own, nor of any effort; yet everything turns out as it should.

Nature creates all beings without erring: this is its straightness. It is calm and still: this is its foursquareness. It tolerates all creatures equally: this is its greatness. Therefore it attains what is right for all without artifice or special intentions. Man achieves the height of wisdom when all that he does is as self-evident as what nature does.

—2nd Hexagram, "The Receptive," The I Ching

Now that a few "illustrations" have been given of what has been called the "solidification" of the world, there remains the question of its representation in geometric symbolism, wherein it can be figured as a gradual transition from sphere to cube. . . . Stability thus understood and represented by the cube, is therefore related to the substantial pole of manifestation, just as immutability in which all possibilities are comprehended in the "global" state represented by the sphere is related to the essential pole. . . .

—René Guenon

XI

Quadrillions

We decided to walk down to Bishop's House. We took the shortcut down the narrow path, which was overhung on both sides with tall fuchsia hedges still in bloom. The path leads down to the main street of Iona, along which the fishermen's cottages have stood facing the sea for centuries. The thatched roofs of old were supplanted by corrugated metal and later by slate. Such a house was now for sale at an enormous price. Two men were working on it, whistling on their ladders and tap-tapping away. We peeked in the bare window and enviously saw the small coziness within. Each of these houses has a walled garden across the road facing St. Ronan's Bay, and you could see how different people chose to arrange them. In the middle of this row of houses stands the Argyll Hotel, which stays open all year. Its garden seemed public enough for us to venture in and sit on a bench without trespassing.

We were feeling lazy that day, and so we sat with our legs outstretched, admiring our identical rubber boots. We were also wearing identical jackets in different colors and identical knitted wool hats with polar bears on them—yours blue and white and mine red and white. We both had cromags or Woodstocks. I could see why people smiled at us. We must have looked like salt and pepper shakers.

The previous day while we were walking hand in hand, we passed a young couple, also walking hand in hand. We smiled at each other. Later that day, we found a letter waiting for us from that couple. In it they had both written a message of regret that they had not met us in person, and they prayed that they would be as happy in each other's company as we seemed to be. May their wish come true!

"What about three dimensions?" you asked out of the blue. "If the shape of three is a triangle and the first enclosed space, how do you get upstairs, so to speak?"

"What would be the smallest number of sides a solid could have?"

"It would have to be four, I suppose. That's odd, isn't it? It takes four to make three dimensions, and three to make two, and two to make one."

"You sound just like Pythagoras," I laughed. "You know, he came up with the idea of the tetractys, a triangle made of ten dots." I bent over and punched ten holes in the ground before us, which was worn clear by people's feet. It looked like this:

"Can you see that you start out with one dot at the top? Then you have two dots to make the first line. This makes a first triangle. Then you add another line of three dots, which make another triangle. With the next four dots you can make a tetrahedron, a three-sided pyramid. If you look at the tetractys and imagine you are looking straight down at it, the center dot of the tetractys makes the apex of the pyramid. It would look like this:

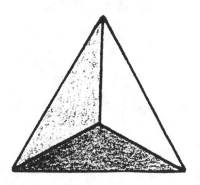

The center dot is looking down at four dots on three sides. So it proves that you have to have four to make three dimensions. *Tetrahedron* means four sides. It is the first solid possible in three dimensions."

You looked dubious. "It doesn't look that solid to me. I think of something really solid as looking like a cube. But that has six sides, doesn't it? We must have skipped one."

"We skipped the four-sided pyramid. That has everything: points, triangles, and a square to boot. Like the Great Pyramid."

"I never thought I could skip over the Great

Pyramid," you teased. "How many of these solids are there?"

"Five. The Great Pyramid is really half an octahedron, so it doesn't count."

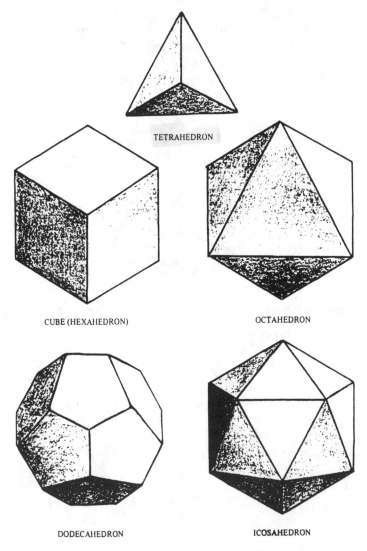

TETRAHEDRON

CUBE (HEXAHEDRON)

OCTAHEDRON

DODECAHEDRON

ICOSAHEDRON

"Let's talk about squares," you said. "I don't think I'm up to pyramids yet. I know already, having been in the one at Gizeh, that there is so much to learn about them and so many books written about them that I feel like an idiot."

"I know what you mean," I agreed, with a heartfelt sigh. "This whole subject of sacred geometry is so enormously important, it staggers the mind. It seems to be the key to everything, to almost all the symbols there are. That's why, it's good to go back to the tetractys and ponder it some more. With ten dots it contains all the numbers 1 through 9, and 10 to grow on. And on and on."

"So let's get back to square one," you said. "That feels both solid and fourish to me."

"Squares sure do. Squares are said to be symbolic of matter and manifestation. They are the four 'whats' that get moved by the three 'hows.' They represent quantity rather than quality, like the four basic elements of old: fire, air, water, and earth; or the building blocks of hydrogen, nitrogen, oxygen, and carbon; or the four directions; or action, thought, emotion, and form; or Jung's four functions of intuition, sensation, thought, and feeling; or the four horsemen of the Apocalypse; or—"

"That's enough!" you protested.

"Oh, but it isn't. I once looked up the number four in Jung's *General Index* and found over a hundred and fifty different entries, just for four, mind you. There were tons more on squares and quaternities. Jung really was interested in threes and fours from every possible symbolic and psychological point of view."

"Do you remember them all?" you teased.

"Are you kidding?" I laughed. "But you can save

a few pages in the notebook to enter them into, as you think of them."

"Hmmmm," you frowned. "It's interesting, though —if you put a cross into a square, you get four smaller squares. That's what squaring means. It's the first number that divides itself in half, into twos. We couldn't do that before. It's the first number that isn't prime."

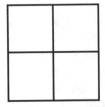

"You know, cities are symbolized by that kind of square. Not only do they have squares, but they used to be divided into 'quarters.' We speak of the Latin Quarter in Paris or of the financial quarter of any city. Most ancient cities and towns were traditionally built in squares and provided market squares for commerce. Unlike circles, the areas of squares are easily measured. The word *market* is cognate with *marking*, with the *mark* as a unit of money, and all of those words with Mercury, the patron god of com*merce*."

"It sure seems like one of Sophia's games is etymology," you chuckled. You were right.

We went on to ponder why, in both the East and the West, odd numbers were considered masculine and even numbers feminine. When I researched the matter later, I discovered it was for anatomical reasons. *I* was phallic and *II* vaginal. I also discovered that the Arabs counted twelve orifices in the male body, but thirteen in the female. Oddly enough, the sun appears to take twelve months to travel the year or the zodiac, but the moon may have thirteen lunations in the same span of time. "And guess how many golf balls you can stick around a central ball and have them all touch?"

"Twelve," you answered. "I had a dodecahedron calendar on my desk once. But if thirteen is an odd number, how can it be feminine?"

"I wondered about that, too. But after the number 10, you add the digits to bring them back to their essence. 13 is 1 + 3·which equals 4, and that's an even number. Maybe the spiritual application of that is that the moon, and the feminine, have something to do with manifestation. Who knows?"

"Well," you joked, "you just said that four is the result of putting two and two together. Ha!" Then you added the observation that with the double digits after ten, they all reverse odds and evens, until 20. With the 30's it repeats the 10's. We agreed that numbers were certainly most intriguing.

We had to move suddenly to the edge of the road as a small freckled-faced boy whizzed by on his bicycle. He looked so pleased with himself and the world, it was contagious.

You went on speculating. "Squares suggest cubes to me. They have another dimension, with height, breadth, and length. Aha! So that's why it is symbolic of matter—because the material world has three dimensions. It makes sense."

"The ancient Chinese had the same idea. In fact, they dressed their emperors in circular tops with squared off bottoms to their robes for that very reason."

"You mean the wisdom was supposed to trickle down? Maybe that's why we have round heads and consider being called a 'square head' an insult. Boy, the things all this leads to," you laughed and shook your round head.

"If the circle is symbolic of spirit and the square is symbolic of matter, you can see why 'squaring the circle' was such a big deal. Squaring the circle is the ongoing *process* of manifestation, individuation, and incarnation. It would argue against materialism on a logical basis because you can't square a circle without a circle. The circle is implied, remember, with every cross. There is a cross hidden in every square. A circle is implicate, and a square is explicate. A circle is one, infinite, and a square is two by two and definite. One can be measured and the other cannot."

"You've lost me," you protested. I have to think it through, step by step. I thought squaring the circle was impossible."

"It is, unless you hear the expression symbolically. Only then does it make sense. It's not really a math problem. It's more, I think, about making the invisible visible."

"What is really meant by *individuation*?" you asked.

"That was Jung's term for self-realization, which he believed was the secret agenda or the ultimate goal of every person coming into this world. He remarked one day that individuation theologically understood is incarnation—a person becoming as total a human being in the flesh as is possible.

Theologically, it means God becoming human; and Christ himself said to his disciples, 'Ye are gods.' "

"But how many people realize this is their purpose?"

"Perhaps it takes more than one lifetime to see it. Who can tell? But Jung meant what all the Teachers have implied: that the unexamined life is not worth living, for then it remains mostly unconscious and almost a waste in terms of what it could have been. But I really cannot imagine anything in nature really being wasted," I hastened to add. "Nature recycles."

"Is it ever too late?" you wondered.

"Not according to the parable of 'The Laborers in the Vineyard.' They got the same wages, though they arrived late in the day. Remember the Self knows no time or space. They are in the realm of the ego."

You stopped to smell a peach-colored rose that was hanging over a wall. "Mmmmm!" you murmured appreciatively. Then you continued. "When you talk about 'incarnation,' are you referring to Christ?"

"I think I am referring to the process of life taking on material form, which Christ's Incarnation in Jesus symbolizes. Incarnation refers to all life that has form, religious persuasion aside. It is such a mystery and such a wonder that life, which is invisible, becomes visible in form. The Incarnation of love may be what the Teachers, and Jesus especially, are pointing to as our next task."

We walked along in silence, neither one of us very satisfied with humanity's progress in this direction, yet not wishing to say so.

You shook your head. "Cheer up," you said. "I just had another thought. What is the three-dimensional version of a circle?" As if you didn't know!

"A sphere."

"All right. So wouldn't you say that volume of a sphere is the same in three dimensions as the area of a circle is in two? They both measure content.

"Well, think of it—the cubic content or volume of a cube or three-dimensional square can be measured accurately. That's the pride and joy of the materialist, right? But what about the volume of a sphere? What's the formula for that?"

I shook my head in shame. I had totally forgotten it. I looked at you hopefully.

"I think I can remember it from school. They drilled it into us. 'Multiply the cube of the radius by pi, multiply by four, and divide by three.' It looks something like this":

$$\frac{r^3 \times pi \times 4}{3}$$

"Glory be!" I exclaimed, mainly because the implication should set any materialist back. "The mystery still remains because of pi. So you cannot explain or measure *everything*; you can only come close. The whole really *is* greater than its parts."

You came to a stop, looked up, and closed your eyes, fishing for the right words. "Well," you said solemnly, "listen to this. If the radius of the circle is 'the Only Way' and you cube the 'Only Way,' symbolically speaking, you are saying that you become whole or individuated by living the 'Only Way' in three dimensions! That is the intention of the Self—to become whole. But in order to do this in the manifest world, we have to act (multiply) and examine (divide)."

I was stunned at that point. "What about the four and the three?"

"The four," you said, "stands for the quantitative world, and the three for the qualitative. So the formula suggests that we have to manifest our lives and then extract the meaning of them."

"What about pi?" I asked, trying hard to follow you. My brain felt like a pretzel at that moment.

"Pi is one of Sophia's secret weapons."

"Maybe it's one of God's jokes," I thought. I knew that pi to the ancient mathematicians was a sacred secret. One had to be initiated even to hear of it. The builders of the Great Pyramid in Egypt had known of it. The three and the four are united in that pyramid: four triangles set upon a square of thirteen acres.

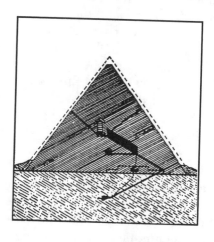

It had been a remarkable conversation, to say the least. I felt that you had suggested something that I would have to ponder on for a long time. It spoke volumes, not areas. Areas are for discussion and measurement; volumes are something far greater. Volumes suggested fullness, a fullness of life and spirit hidden within the sphere of the psyche. A fullness trying to transform the *prima materia* within it.

I was reminded suddenly of myself as a child in boarding school in Italy, struggling with an assignment to memorize the words of St. Paul: "That Christ may dwell in your hearts, that ye being rooted and grounded in love may be able to comprehend with all the saints what is the breadth, and length, and depth and height. . . ." There I got stuck, but I knew it had to do with knowing that love that passes understanding so that we can be filled with the fullness of God. It all took on new meaning for me.

I now had a new perception of both the circle and the sphere, and later I tried to draw it. I could do the circle, which became the sun full of rays. But drawing the sphere was beyond me. In my mind's eye I saw a dandelion, which is a golden disk of rays at one stage and a perfect sphere filled with luminous white radii at another. We call them weeds! They are miraculous teachers strewn beneath our feet.

I shared this with you, and you agreed. The one radius for "the Only Way" was a singled-out example. Actually we apply that process, or can, in an infinitude of directions.

Then I had another funny memory. A fellow student of M's, a middle-aged woman, was enormously enthusiastic about everything. She had learned a meditation technique where you try to identify and "be" a plant. Soon she had us all sitting in a row "being" cabbages. The results were hilarious, and I must say I developed a respect for that vegetable which I have held ever since.

I decided that feeling like the diademed sphere of a dandelion would be an extraordinary experience.

I would not even mind being "blown away." The thought made me pensive, because already I knew that such a meditation would have to be centered in the heart. This led to a childhood memory of Italy and what I considered atrociously designed little cards of the Sacred Heart of Jesus. But now I could see in them the irrational notion of radiating love. In my childish snobbery, I had totally missed the point. Symbols do not represent; they point the way. As the Sufis say, they are theophanies of the absolute in the relative. *Theophany* in Greek means a "showing forth of God." I felt humbly grateful for this new insight, and ashamed of myself at the same time.

Synchronicity did not fail on this occasion. As we walked on past Bishop's House, we came across several dandelions. School was out, and we overtook some children playing ball. The relentless etymologist in me came up with the origin of *ball*. It is thought to be *Bel*, the name meaning "Son of El" or Son of the Lord. The Beltane fires of May Day of the Celts were connected to the ball of the sun. The sun radiates. So we come back to the radii of the circle, which Jung speaks of as the center and totality of the human psyche.

By the same token, each of us is perhaps a radius of the great mystery lying at the center of creation. It is the process (verb) that is concealed in all creation: luminous, radiant love. Could this be the symbolic, indefinable mystery of pi?

With that last crazy notion, I swept into the hotel through the door, behind you. We could smell recent baking, and sure enough it was time again for tea in the lounge. The cups were laid out, the water samovar gleaming and purring, and an assortment of delectable buttered scones, strawberry jam, various cakes and biscuits were laid out on the table. We carried our steaming cups to some armchairs and stared out the large windows at the view of the mountains of Mull across the water. There was a discreet sound of tinkling teaspoons around the room and a soft murmur of friendly voices. I don't know if it was from the hot tea or from the over-flowing of gratitude, but I could feel my heart shining and radiating with inner warmth and just plain love of living. It was like living on the edge of some great truth—implied, implicated, folded within. I spread out the small white square of my paper napkin. For an instant, it bore the imprint of the face of God.

Everything the Power of the World does is done in a circle. The sky is round, and I have heard that the earth is round like a ball, and so are all the stars. The wind, in its greatest power, whirls. Birds make their nests in circles, for theirs is the same religion as ours. The sun comes forth and goes down again in a circle. The moon does the same, and both are round. Even the seasons form a great circle in their changing. . . . The life of man is a circle from childhood to childhood, and so it is in everything where power moves. Our tepees were round like the nests of birds, and were always set in a circle, the nation's hoop, a nest of many nests, where the Great Spirit meant for us to hatch our children.

—John Neihardt

Heaven's way is round, earth's way is square.

—Lu Wu-pei (Chinese poet)

Wherefore the Lord says in a mystery: "Except ye make the things of the right as those of the left, and those of the left as those of the right, and those that are above, as those below, and those that are behind as those that are before, ye shall not have knowledge of the kingdom."

—The Apocryphal New Testament

The Pythagoreans thought that this [the square] more than any other four-sided figure carries the image of the divine nature. It is their favorite figure for indicating immaculate worth; for the rightness of the angles imitates integrity, and the equality of the sides abiding power. . . . Philolaus, moreover, in another of his reflections calls the angle of the square the angle of Rhea, Demeter, and Hestia. For since the square is the substance of earth, as we learn from [Plato's] Timaeus and since the earth receives powers from these goddesses, he rightly dedicates the angle of the square to these life-giving forces.

—Proclus

The number One is hidden in all numbers.

—Mercy Muchmore

XII
Cubes within Cubes

After tea we went back to our room to rest a while and read. Our room was down a corridor in a part of the hotel somewhat isolated from the main section, so we did not hear the commotion of the arrival of one of the "lama-lama" groups that periodically descend upon Iona like a flock of exotic birds. *Lama-lama* is an affectionate word, coined by one of my daughters, to describe generically the kind of folk interested in alternative ways of being. She first used it in my presence as she tried to describe her mother's interests to one of her friends. Her face screwed up with the effort, and finally she just threw up her hands and cried, "Lama-lama stuff! *You* know what I mean." We all burst out laughing, and the descriptive adjective quickly entered the family vocabulary.

When we entered the lounge before dinner, the noise had gone up by decibels. Loud voices, and gales of laughter filled the room. Blue jeans and sweatsuits, new Aran sweaters on the American men, Indian scarves and huge earrings on the women had replaced the demure tweed skirts and acrylic jerseys

179

of the grey-haired British ladies and the proper tweed jackets of the silver-haired gentlemen. The latter had taken refuge, edged out entirely, in a separate glassed-off room. They sat there sipping their sherry and their Scotch, trying not to seem fascinated by the invasion. The new group was not only American; they came all the way from California.

We stood there briefly with divided loyalties. We had lost our privileged peace as unobtrusive aliens among the older guests, but we, too, were Americans and had even lived in California at one point. It was easy to recognize the vitality, the enthusiasm, the openness and wide-eyed joy our compatriots felt at being really, truly on Iona.

As it happened, there was not a seat left among them, so with friendly smiles all around, we made our way into the glassed-off room to sit with our former peers. Since you and I had both grown up in Europe, we understood both ways of being. The old world and the new have so much to exchange, and the history of Iona makes it a natural nexus for this to happen.

Sipping slowly on a drink, I mused that Moses was a bridge between the wisdom of Egypt and the Jewish nation; Gautama Buddha was a bridge between Hinduism and Buddhism; Jesus was a bridge between Judaism and the gentile world; St. Columba was a bridge between Druidism and Celtic Christianity. Now here was a whole generation bridging an old worldview with a new worldview. The Iona Community, now settled around the abbey and founded by George MacLeod, God bless him, is a perfect example of a steady organization, concerned with brotherly love and world community, through which there is a constant cycling of people coming and going. It is Christ-centered, ecumenical, and concerned with world peace and justice. The lama-lama groups, (and I have seen quite a few come and go on Iona over the years), all have something in common as well—a burning idealism and a sincere desire to change the way things are. I am reasonably certain that some of the other hotel guests might have viewed them as crazies. Had they known more about us, they would have deemed us crazy, too. Yet, as I looked at their good British faces, I suspected that they also had deep reasons for being just where they were. They just weren't so loud about it. Nothing, of course, was said. They knew that we were Americans, and they would never have offended us by being openly critical.

For me, it was an interesting situation. I found myself thinking that had Columba not come to Iona from Ireland, Scotland would not have been converted to Christianity. Had Columba not had disciples who fanned out all over Europe bringing learning (which had flourished in Ireland through the Dark Ages), the future American culture would have been severely diminished. Now here, generations later, Americans had returned to Iona from across the great Atlantic and a great continent Columba never dreamt of—to refresh themselves spiritually. These were some of my thoughts when the dinner gong sounded and we all trooped in to a supper of curried lamb and rice, followed by a trifle pudding.

We truly have no way of knowing how far the influence of one person can travel through space or across time. Those radiating lines of light seem to go forth from one psyche for centuries. They can fall on a seed of intention in another soul and bring it suddenly to green life. As Lao Tzu said, a wise person can sit in his room and affect someone three thousand miles away—or down through the ages.

I looked at the sensible guests around us and thought of the lama-lamas in the next room, and it seemed almost as if each of us sits at the center of an outspreading web of potential affect.

There is a curious mathematical progression that is weblike. We have two parents, four grandparents, eight great-grandparents, and so on back, always doubling through time. The same sequence occurs as the human fetus is formed in the uterus by the process of mitosis: 2, 4, 8, 16 cells, and on and on. There seems to be some connection—one web is outer stretching through a multitude of ancestors and the other web is inner, a recondensing of past generations. The nexus is where they meet and become one at conception. I find this fascinating.

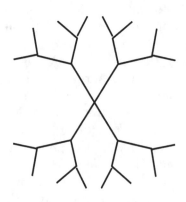

Multiplicity, or the world of "ten thousand things," is centrifugal. The necessity of finding meaning in all this multiplicity within ourselves comes through yoking the opposites, putting two and two back together inside ourselves. This effort is centripetal in motion, moving us back to the center. We breathe in the world with our first breath, and breathe out the world with our last one. Perhaps the reflexive opposite is what happens within us. We breathe our spirit out into the world with our individual intentions, and breathe in the values of our experience. The word *spiritus*, part of re*spir*ation, means "breath." *Holy Spirit*, means "Holy Breath." *Sophia* means "Holy Breathing."

The body, which is our world encyclopedia, lives by breathing in oxygen and breathing out carbon dioxide, and some mysterious circulations in the four chambers of the heart exchange blue venous blood for red arterial blood. The anonymous author of the profoundly Christian *Meditations on the Tarot* speaks of horizontal and vertical breathing. He writes:

> There are two kinds of respiration: horizontal respiration which takes place between "outside" and "inside," and vertical respiration which takes place between "above" and "below." The "sting of death" or the essential crisis of the supreme agony is the abrupt passage from horizontal to vertical respiration. Yet he who has learnt vertical respiration whilst living will be spared from this "sting of death." For him the passage from one form of respiration to the other will not be of the nature of a right angle but rather the arc of a circle. The transition will not be abrupt but gradual, and curved instead of rectangular.

I was struck especially by the idea that such breathing transforms angles into arcs. ("That's why it's arcane!" interrupted Mercy Muchmore. She's impossible.) Psychologically speaking, I would assume vertical breathing to be the exchange between ego and Self—the kind of yogic breathing undertaken in meditation which affects the chakra system or the inner cycling and recycling of knowledge into wisdom. The ego offers up its experience and consciousness, and the Self blesses us with insights and Ahas!, with the grace of more inwit.

It is perhaps in this "Only Way" that the psyche can accomplish the mystery from the Apocrypha quoted at the head of this chapter, which Jung mentions in his "Transformational Symbolism in the Mass." Making left and right, above and below, behind and before, one describes a cube.

Now comes the tricky part. If you build a cube of cubes, 3 x 3 x 3 or 3 to the third power, you get a block of 27 cubes. This is much bigger than the cubed one of 2 x 2 x 2, which gives only 8.

Were we to paint the 3 cubed one bright red, we would have:

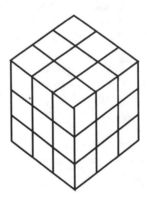

6 small cubes painted red on 1 side
12 small cubes painted red on 2 sides
8 small cubes painted red on 3 sides

If you add these together you get 26 cubes with color. But there are 27 cubes in all. Where is the 27th cube? It is the one at the center; it is uncolored, and *it is in contact with every other cube in the whole block.*

So what?

Sophia would have us take that fourth step and look for a spiritual implication. The central cube, like the Self, is present and contiguous in the three-dimensional world, though it remains different and invisible. It is just so.

This can be profoundly comforting (Paraclete) as we shoulder our way through the seemingly impervious material world. Even on the darkest day, when all the world seems obdurate, it is good to think of that secret wee cube sitting hidden in the blocks confronting one. And to know that even if we feel like a blockhead there's hope.

Contemplating such a cube, we find again a demonstration of the interaction of 3s and 4s (qualities and quantities). As with the sphere, each cube contains a hidden center, a center that Jung tells us is the only place where we transcend the world. The center cube is patently in the world, but not of it. So we need not deny the world, as we have for generations been told to do. We can embrace the world and dwell securely within it by remaining conscious that we too have a hidden Divine Guest, symbolized here by the one precious cube, different and yet like, which contains within *itself* the point of no dimension, the bindu, the seed of our eternal being.

An interesting fact brings this analogy close to home. Salt crystals are cubes (to the alchemist, salt was symbolic of Sophia), and so, I am told, are gold crystals, which are symbolic of the sun, both outer and inner.

The cube plays a great part in the wisdom of the Kabbalah. There each face and edge and point is given a special significance. But I promised to keep this simple, as simple as a child's building block.

Absurdly, sitting there, I remembered how struck I was one summer when I was fifteen. I had been reading William James's *Varieties of Religious Experience*. In the book was an example of how helpful the image of a cube can be to someone trying to overcome alcoholism or any other addiction. James suggested that trying to overcome an addiction is like lifting a heavy cube which threatens to fall back on one. But once you get it teetering on edge and finally push it over, the temptation is gone for good. The struggle lies in lifting it over.

All the while as these thoughts were tumbling through my mind, I thought of my experiments building with sugar cubes back home. They were sweet, but not as sweet as the great Aha!s that they taught me.

I had to laugh. You wondered what the joke was, and I said it was one of those complicated ones. Even now, I am struggling and wondering if any of this makes sense to anyone else. Oh, Sophia, what are you doing to me?

It was after dinner, and the American lama-lama group was now ensconced in the smaller partitioned lounge for lectures. We were invited to join them, which we did. The lecture was excellent, but the weary pilgrims who had come such a distance in that one day (or were they already under the spell of Iona?) one by one nodded off or spaced out with their inner thoughts, as I found myself constantly doing on the island. Sophia's dove was wafting them away. There was peace in the room, and the voice of the lecturer murmured on like a brook finding its way through the night. The faces, young and old, looked blissed out, as well they should.

We crept out with a grateful nod to the speaker, and wended our way through the other lounge of the sensible back to our own room and our bed. It had been another full day.

Listen, O dearly beloved!
I am the reality of the world, the center of the circumference,
I am the parts and the whole.
I have created perception in you only in order to be the object
of my perception. . . .
Dearly beloved!
I have called you so often and you have not heard me.
I have shown myself to you so often and you have not seen me.
I have made myself fragrance so often and you have not
smelled me,
Savorous food, and you have not tasted me.
Why can you not reach me through the object you touch?

    —Ibn al Arabi, 13th Century Sufi scientist and mystic

Plato considered geometry and number as the most reduced
and essential, and therefore the ideal, philosophical
language. But it is only by virtue of functioning at a certain
"level" of reality that geometry and number can become a
vehicle for philosophic contemplation. Greek philosophy
defined this notion of "levels," so useful in our thinking,
distinguishing the "typal" and the "archetypal." . . . The
archetypal is concerned with universal processes or dynamic
patterns which can be considered independently of any
structure or material form. Modern thought has difficult
access to the concept of the archetypal because European
languages require that verbs or action words be associated
with nouns. We therefore have no linguistic forms with
which to image a process or activity that has no material
carrier. Ancient cultures symbolized these pure, eternal
processes as gods, that is, powers or lines of action through
which Spirit is concretized into energy and matter.

    —Robert Lawlor

Only subjective [ego] consciousness is isolated; when it
relates to its centre it is integrated into wholeness . . . if
you can see and understand your suffering without being
subjectively involved, then, because of your altered
standpoint, you also understand "how not to suffer."

    —C. G. Jung

XIII
The Golden Rectangle

We had planned an interlude during our visit to Iona to return to another favorite place, the Isle of Skye. Skye lies to the north of Iona and is a long day's journey, when you count the ferry rides and the drive through some of the most spectacular glens in Scotland.

Skye is much bigger than Iona in every way. It is over forty miles long and is filled with high mountains, the Black and the Red Cuillins. Called the Isle of Mists, Skye shimmers and sways almost constantly under showers and rainbows. It is an island of moods; I have never seen it twice the same. For the visitor, it has everything: ruined castles, mountain-climbing, pony-trekking, wool-gathering, brochs and standing stones, shops (a few), and comfortable lodgings.

We chose to stay in Sligachan, midway up the island on the east coast. Our hotel room overlooked a river that plummeted over large grey rocks, under an old bridge, and out to a narrow loch or fjord. I feel that I can use the Norse term *fjord*, since the Hebrides were all once under the rule of Norwegian kings. In fact, you can see a little bump on top of

189

one of the red Cuillins. It is the cairn over the grave of a Norwegian princess, who, so homesick was she, asked to be buried there so the breezes of her homeland would blow over her grave.

On this day we chose to visit the coral beach, which curves around a very small bay just beyond Dunvegan Castle, the seat of the MacLeods. The castle, still inhabited by the same family, has been around over nine hundred years. It is open to visitors and has everything from a dungeon off the living room, to a Fairy Flag, a tattered silk banner given by the fairies to the clan good for three wishes for protection (they have used two). There is a huge horn flagon from which the heir apparent to the chieftanship has to drink claret at one go upon reaching his majority, a feat recently accomplished by John, the MacLeod of MacLeods in the presence of Queen Elizabeth II. I have been to the castle so frequently that I think I know every room by heart. So on to the beach.

After passing several heather-covered hills, we edged our rented car down through muddy sections and parked within walking distance. We could see the turquoise water already, a clear color I have seen only off Greece and in the Bahamas. Here was a genuine coral beach in the Hebrides! It is a geological fluke, formed of broken sea shells, and it gleams surprisingly, luminously white.

Immediately, we were captivated by these jewels of the sea. On Iona it is the stones that are the jewels. Here it is the infinite number of seashells of every kind. Not all were broken, and the search was on to find miniscule whelks, limpets, and sea snails, and the tiny fans of scallops, some orange, some white, some grey. Soon our hands and pockets were full of miracles of geometric design. Every single one revealed a pattern by a master mathematician. Sophia is in her glory here.

We crunched around—there was no sand—until we were worn out with stooping over our wet boots. Finally, we sat down to rest and show off our treasures.

My favorite was a tiny, delicate violet sea snail and yours a coral-colored scallop, smaller than my smallest fingernail. We marveled and marveled. The spiral of mine was as perfect as that of the much larger shell I had at home.

"I wonder how the old mathematicians discovered the laws that govern these designs," you asked. "It seems incredible."

"I don't know," I replied. "Perhaps it had something to do with their way of looking at things. They didn't have a zero or numerals, 1, 2, 3, etc., the way we do; they used letters. Alpha for 1, beta for 2, and so forth. (You can see these in the appendix.) So for them language and quantities overlapped. You can see how the ideas behind numerology, or what the Kabbalists call *gematria* started, because each letter of the alphabet had a numerical value. I have read that during those centuries B.C., people worked geometry by drawing with a stick on a flat board covered with fine sand or placing pebbles or counters on this board. It was called an *abacus*, from the Semitic word *abq*, which means 'dust.' When they calculated (*calculus* means 'pebble') arithmetically, they drew vertical lines like this:

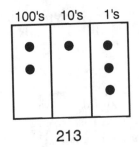

213

"That's how the abacus with beads was generated, and it's still used all over the world."

"Yes, I remember the one we saw them using in the shop in Moscow," you said.

I tried to demonstrate the ancient way by scratching in the coral and putting larger stones in place. "You can see that if you put three stones in a triangle, it is the shape of the idea or concept of three. Or four—" and I made a little square with four pebbles. "Perhaps for them the medium was the message—the two weren't separated. You remember Archimedes was killed by a Roman soldier in Syracuse while he was drawing in the sand."

" '*Noli turbare circulos meos!* ' " you quoted. " 'Don't disturb my circles!' but he was killed anyway."

At this point we got off on the subject of Archimedes, who is best remembered for being a "Eureka streaker," after discovering the way to calculate volume through the displacement of water in his bathtub.

You reminded me of his inventiveness. "He was the Werner von Braun of his time. He destroyed the Roman fleet off Sicily by focusing huge mirrors on the sails of their ships and causing them to burst into flames. He invented a grappling hook which could lift up an enemy boat from one end and cause everyone and everything to tumble off into the sea, which must have been very humiliating. The Romans could have used him on their side! And he invented the hydraulic screw and all kinds of useful mechanical things. He was really a genius."

"Well, by his time geometry was being used for science and technology, as it is today. But it was not always so. Even later in the Middle Ages, as woodcuts show, the figures of Geometria and Arithmetica were personified as women, Sophias, involved with the philosophical aspect of both subjects. In front of them are men working to make these pure concepts practical.

"In ancient times, the philosophers (lovers of Sophia) weren't thinking about weapons or apples and eggs and the grocery bill. They were finding proofs of divine order, and, as far as I'm concerned, they found them. But I think the next step for us, since today we are almost lost in materialism, is to use the material to prove the spiritual. We can look at the marvel and secrets of apples and eggs and see that they contain revelations and proofs sitting right there on the kitchen table. Just think of what you find when you cut an apple in two, sideways—stop and think."

You closed your eyes and thought. "I don't normally cut an apple that way. I don't know. But, believe it or not, I have one in my pocket. I saved it from breakfast." You pulled out a bright green apple, and I hugged my knees with delight. You took out your Swiss army knife, and carefully bisected it horizontally. Together we looked at the result. In the middle of the apple was a perfect little pentagram.

I grinned at your surprise. "You wouldn't think that that little pentagram makes the apple related geometrically to this tiny shell, but it does."

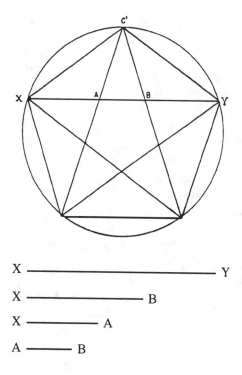

I explained that both designs are connected to the Golden Rectangle—the pentagram through its proportions, and the shell through its pattern of growth. The properties engendered by the proportions of this special rectangle are truly extraordinary. Something wonderful and new was added with this rectangle: motion. It's made of whirling squares. You have to move it to make it work. So much in nature is connected to it, we have to study it.

"I don't know how the ancient geometers ever figured it out, but they did. Of all the mysteries of sacred geometry, this one is one of the most spectacular—at least to me. It is a place where the human mind connects a mathematical abstraction with a law of nature, and they coincide.

"I first learned about it from M. I still remember sitting at a card table in my small flat in Greenwich Village and working the rectangle out on tracing paper. When I had finished it and drawn the spiral, I placed it over a photograph of a sectioned chambered nautilus shell—and the spirals fit! This tiny shell," and I pointed to the little sea snail in your hand, "is a mathematical miracle.

"It boggled my mind that such a thing is possible. I don't know which was more miraculous, the shell's perfect design or the fact that the human mind was capable of finding the formula for it so long ago. It is for me the grand climax, the masterpiece of geometry, because not only does it involve the Golden Rectangle and the proportions of the pentagram, but also the Fibonacci series of numbers, and the so-called E-curve of growth."

"Good grief!" you muttered, spitting out an apple pip, as you began eating the apple. "How do you draw one?"

"Well, I suppose we will have to do it in our books. I couldn't do it on the ground here. You really need a straight edge and a compass. But it is not that difficult."

So we agreed to wait. On the way back, we stopped for tea at a recently constructed tea shop run by the people at the castle. I thought compassionately of the prisoners of the past who had been thrown down into the wide well of the dungeon of the MacLeods, and how the guide had once explained that there was a tube set in the wall to the kitchen, so prisoners could smell the food while they starved to death. A very practical arrangement disposed of the bodies. A sea-gate opened and let the tide wash them out into oblivion. And there we were, genteely stirring the sugar in our teacups and nibbling on fresh scones and jam!

In the parking lot, we interrupted a number of colorful chaffinches pecking around hopefully for crumbs. They looked like sparrows dressed up for Mardi Gras. I picked up a single feather fallen near the rear bumper. It, too, was a miracle of shadings. When I showed it to you, you reminded me of the Japanese scientist who became converted to religion in a moment of satori as he gazed at a bird feather, realizing that it was designed to rest between the other feathers in just such a way as to provide a set sequence in a pattern—a pattern common to all the other birds of that species.

We discussed this at length during the spectacular drive back to Sligachan. Before us was a fairy tale scene of tall, peaked black mountains, with swirls of mist brooding on their tops. First you see them from afar, and then the road curves away and brings you back to a closer, and then an even closer view. The effect is overwhelming. You can see readily how the original inhabitants of Skye millennia ago conjured up tales of giants and warrior gods and goddesses and dramas filled with supernatural wonders. In fact, to this day there is strong belief in the supernatural and ghosts and the Wee Folk in the Hebrides. This is not hard to understand, given the setting. These mountains were the home of the goddess Scatach[Sciath] who ran a school for heroes. Finally, one of her most able students, Cu Chulainn (of Irish fame) overwhelmed her. The result was motherhood.

We debated the question of the immanence of divinity, by whatever name you wish to call it. So much beauty is to be found in the world, so much more than is necessary. And the more science pushes out to the macrocosm of space or into the microcosm of the atomic world, the more harmony, design, and wonder there is to discover. There are even little creatures in the water, a kind of plankton called radiolaria that are shaped according to the five Platonic solids! (See the appendix for some pictures.)

I remembered the first time that I read Lawrence Blair's wonderful book *Rhythms of Vision*. I was shocked to learn the following about the shape and proportions of the DNA molecule, which carries the genetic code in every cell of our bodies:

> The chemical model for these proteins consists of two-dimensional platelets of two fused pairs of hexagons and pentagons joined by a 'golden mean' rectangle, which rise upon each other in a three-dimensional spiral.

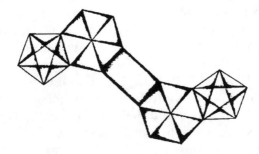

This means that we carry these very patterns everywhere in ourselves, but we never knew it until Drs.

Watson and Crick discovered the genetic code in the early 1950s.

I tried to put this into words as we drove along. I was close to tears of frustration at my lack of appropriate vocabulary and knowledge. You put your hand out on my arm to calm me down.

"The wonder of the genetic code for me," you said, "is that, first of all, whatever we consume on any level always turns into who we are. If we share the same bread or drink the same wine or look at the same sunset, it always turns into you or me. We are a bit like holographs, aren't we. Every part of us describes the whole. At that rate, we are sharing a process with divinity—we are microcosms doing the same thing, perhaps, that God is doing. All of creation —and I mean galaxies and everything out there and in here—is like the genetic code of God. In that sense, we really are 'created in the image of God.' "

"Well, at least I am beginning to understand better," I confessed, "what they meant about God geometrizing. If one can apply Sophia's fourth step and look for the spiritual implications hidden within these physical symbols, we might end up closer—"

"Closer to what?"

"Awe. That place where reason and intellect fall down upon their knees before the wonder and the splendor of it all." By now I was genuinely in tears. We stopped the car and you held me in your arms. As I am writing this, my eyes are brimming in remembrance. The kingdom of heaven is indeed hidden within this world, though we don't often see it, perhaps because we don't take time. But mostly I think we don't know how. Where are the teachers to teach us how to see?

When we got back to the hotel, we took a much-needed nap. Then we dressed for dinner. We had oysters, cream of leek soup, poached salmon (whether literal or culinary, we could not know), yellow potatoes and peas, cheese and biscuits. We shared the bread and drank some cool wine, and we invited our Divine Guest to partake of the goodness and the richness of the day. We left the drawing of the Golden Rectangle for the next morning.

The next day the weather had changed again. It was raining and blowing in an admirable Scottish way. We took refuge with our copybooks in the lounge called the Tower Room, because it was circular like our room just above it. We found an unused table and set to work on the Golden Rectangle.

Before we began I pointed out that we would have to go from the greater design to the smaller and smaller, because our paper would not allow us to keep getting bigger and bigger. We could end up with a galaxy if we didn't watch out. But it was important to remember that you could go either way.

The first step is to make a square:

The next step is to extend this square by making an arc with the compass set midway on the bottom line of the square and the pencil at the top left corner. With this you sweep an arc. This arc, when completed, gives a point to which the base line of the square can be extended to form a Golden Rectangle:

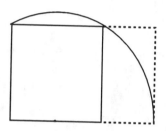

The resulting vertical rectangle (shown with the dotted lines) has exactly the same proportions as the larger horizontal one. Now you mark out a square within the vertical rectangle, using the measurement of the extension. This leaves another Golden Rectangle. This can go on giving smaller and smaller or bigger and bigger Golden Rectangles.

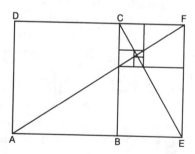

The next step is to join the arcs to form a spiral called the E-curve of growth, because it is the pattern by which tendrils of plants follow as they grow. It also governs the way leaves on a rosebush spiral up so that they do not cast shade upon each other. You find it in the whirl of sunflower seeds, in pine cones, in unfolding ferns, in the swelling forth of life in so many diverse places—a galaxy in outer space, the curve of the embryo and the cowlick on a baby's head:

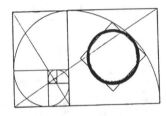

It is this spiral that I once drew for M that fits over the chambered nautilus and that would fit the snail that I now held in my parka pocket. The basic ratio for this exercise is known as phi (ϕ). It states that the smaller term is to the larger term as the larger is to the smaller term plus the larger: $a:b::b: (a+b)$. The great mathematician Fibonacci discovered it in the sequence: 0 1 2 3 5 8 13 21 ... which governs the distribution of many growth patterns in plants: $2+1=3$; $3+2=5$ ... or 5 is to 8 as 8 would be to $8+5$ which is 13.

We stopped to consider our efforts. It is an impressive exercise, believe me. We were in new territory here, discovering relationships or ratios. If we applied Sophia's fourth step, what would the implication be? We pondered some more and then, half-wits that we are, came up with the same insight simultaneously. "Aha!" we cried.

"What?" you asked.

"No, you go first."

"If it keeps on getting bigger or smaller always in the same proportions, isn't that the geometric proof of a certain process?"

"As above, so below?" said I.

"Exactly—it's the way analogies and correspondences work when they are correct. They fit that formula."

"*It is a geometric proof for the value of symbolism.* It says that a symbol can lead to a truth which by extension can lead us to a greater truth. So that's how symbols work. They spiral on up and out to greater and greater insights."

"Can you say more about that?" you asked.

"I'll try. We have to remember that symbols point to processes. They are not emblems, which like business logos point to other *things.* Symbols help move us from one level of understanding to another. Symbolically speaking, the straight lines of the rectangle have to do with the concrete matter at hand, but the spiraling arc or curve leads us to greater and greater insights. A poet might say that a spiral is a circle in the act of growing."

"Give me an example," you challenged.

"Well, take the cup exercise. What is the process symbolized by a cup?"

"Containing, which is a verb."

"Then containing is the symbolic process, the key to a cup as a symbol. By extension to the level of ritual, the cup is related to the chalice. By further symbolic extension to the level of myth, the cup-chalice becomes the Holy Grail. By even further extension to the spiritual level, the cup-chalice-Holy

Grail becomes the divine personification of all containing—Mother Nature or the Mother Goddess.

"In this instance, the symbol has moved us from
the physical reality of a cup on the table to an
archetypal or cosmic principle. The chalice is still
a physical thing, but in a religious setting, it has
become numinous. The Holy Grail in this instance
is mediating in the myth between the visible and the
invisible world, hence the quest for it. It appears
and disappears. It is renewed, according to the
myth, every year by the Dove (of Sophia)."

"Every time we talk about it," you said, "we seem
to find more wisdom in it. The Golden Rectangle
just makes the process more reasonable. For me, it's
like looking into a piece of machinery and seeing
how it works."

I knew instinctively that ancient people expressed
this power of the symbolic. The distinction between
the gods and humans is that the gods or archetypal
processes are immortal, eternal. Containing, in this
instance, is per se an eternal or ongoing process.
So are creating or destroying or recycling and many
other processes basic to life.

The beauty is that these processes can be recognized; there is a symbolic language for them which
has been called "an algebra of life," but few have
recognized it for what it is. Like sacred geometry,
it is still scorned and rejected in many places, yet
it, too, reveals the link between the invisible and
the visible world, the *unus mundus*. That symbolic
language of archetypal processes is, of course,
astrology. When rightly understood astrology is a
philosophical subject that can be studied quite apart
from horoscopes. I find it sad that so few people
understand this, but Jung did.

Thoughtfully, you took a handkerchief out of your pocket and blew your nose. "So what you are saying is, in terms of sacred geometry, the power of the Golden Rectangle is that it, like other symbols, works as a mathematical abstraction in itself, yet also demonstrably implies truths in the realms of nature, the mind, the soul, and the spirit. It moves from the smaller to the greater or from the greater to the smaller, always keeping the same harmonious proportions. That, for me, is a very powerful Aha." You paused and shook your head. "What would you consider to be an example of symbolism on the psychological level?"

"On the psychological level it would have to be a parable or a myth—a singular story having many levels of meaning. This is why the great Teachers spoke in parables, and why myths are universal to all cultures. Myths deal with divinities; fairy tales deal with people encountering archetypal situations and archetypal characters in archetypal places. They all have psychological insights to offer. Jung even said that at the heart of every complex is a god. The Bible and sacred scriptures of other traditions are filled to overflowing with psychological truths. In studying them, we reverse the symbolism of the Golden Rectangle, moving from the spiritual and collective to the needs of an individual person. That's like working the Golden Rectangle from big to small."

At this point, we were interrupted by a waiter rolling in a tray with "elevenses." Coffee was being served. We took a necessary break from the higher verities, and after the coffee went outdoors briefly to watch the torrent of the Sligachan river rush under the bridge. Then we returned to finish up the discussion.

"What about the physical level of the Golden Rectangle?" your ever practical mind spoke out.

"This is where Sophia is most hidden. The geometry of a crystal, of a flower, of a tree, of a wave breaking, of a galaxy whirling can be a key to its hidden significance. The spiraling is the slow ascent to wisdom and insight such natural things can lead us to. They lead us from one level of understanding to another. That is the process by which we learn through symbolic thinking. Symbols really are what the Sufis say: theophanies of the eternal in the relative.

"In nature, the shape of the number is the key, or the number hidden in the shape. In botany, irises go by threes and sixes; strawberries and apples go by fives; snow crystals and beehives go by sixes; and so forth. The numbers involved are called *signatures* by herbalists. Oddly enough, poisonous plants often have seven petals. Each plant unfolds according to the numbers it belongs to. They do not all follow the Golden Rectangle mathematically. Its value for us lies in pointing a way to symbolic thinking and disclosing patterns of growth through correspondences."

"Maybe 'keys' in music are the same," you mused.

"I am sure they are, but I don't know enough to explain it. Pythagoras had the same notion. For instance, he found that if you pinch a harp string at the halfway point, it plays exactly an octave higher. Later he discovered the mathematical proportions of harmonics. Only a few years ago, further experiments showed that sounds in turn make geometric figures called *eidophones*."

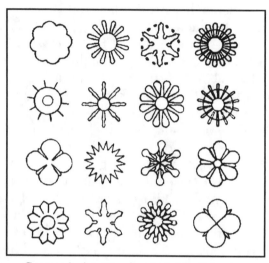

Geometrical patterns produced by the voice
(From Eidophone Voice Figures by Watts Hughes)

One of my favorite examples is Bode's Law. The astronomer Bode discovered that the distances between the planets from the sun to Saturn are proportionate to the distances between notes on a guitar string. To make this work, you have to include the belt of asteroids. Pythagoras anticipated this in "the music of the spheres."

The implications of so many of these correspondences are profound, yet science doesn't follow through with step four, since this is not its province. Religion overlooks the connection as well. Science loses its sense of the sacred, and religion much of its available proof. Yet the bridge between the two, the fulcrum, is there waiting for us. Perhaps this is one of the challenges for the age to come.

Claude Bragdon, an ardent geometer, called architecture "frozen music." He showed how you translate the design of certain buildings into rhythms. He looked at the verticals interrupting the spaces between them. Beautiful structures sing to the eye. Nature creates geometric rhythm spontaneously, but the Egyptians and the Greeks and the Muslims did it by design. And centuries later, after the Dark Ages and the loss of sacred geometry to Western culture, it was recovered in part due to the Crusades, because the Arabs had never lost the knowledge.

"Maybe we've lost it all over again," you noted. "All the modern glassed-in skyscrapers go 1/1/1/1/1 when you look at them. It's sort of architectural rap!" We laughed wryly. There do seem to be very few curves or melodies in contemporary buildings.

We had to stop for lunch and a rest to absorb these thoughts. Then we pressed on.

The next exercise was to see that you could find two *vesica pisces* in those rectangles. This is the same shape that you get from intersecting two circles. These implied fishes are symbolic of Christianity and the Age of Pisces. They hide in the designs of all the Gothic cathedrals built in the Middle Ages, and in the fish head mitre of bishops, and originally in Jesus' injunction to his disciples to be fishers of men.

The next exercise was to draw another Golden Rectangle and to draw in the diagonals.

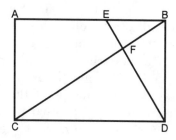

The proportions of the four lines are the same, believe it or not, as those of any pentagram. But that would be for another day. The fascinating thing about those four lines is that every single part of the Parthenon in ancient Athens was built according to those proportions, and many a Christian church centuries later. The result is a truly holy temenos. The message is built in for all time; it is immanent, waiting there for eyes that can perceive.

Today there is a whole new generation of sacred geometers in this century (Schwaller de Lubicz, Keith Critchlow, John Michell, Robert Lawlor, Rachel Fletcher, to name but a few) who are now able to describe for us the mathematical and geometric wonders of ancient Egypt, Greece, pre-Celtic and Celtic Britain, and the medieval sacred architecture.

The weather began to clear. Patches of blue interrupted torn stretches of white clouds. We could see glistening grasses bending under the blowing breeze. We closed our books and set off for Portree, the one central town on Skye and its capital. Here we bought some newspapers and wandered up and down the conveniently short main street. We looked in the windows of the butcher shop, the wool store, the pharmacy, the ironmonger's, the sporting goods store, the newly modernized stationery store, and the superior craft gifts cum bookstore. The needs of the islanders and the needs of the tourists were well met here, and their spiritual needs were met by several churches of different denominations. Huge buses loaded with mostly elderly people from different countries groaned and hissed, as they braked and turned in the small space allotted them in the town square. Everything delighted us, for no particular reason. We enjoyed the ordinariness of the day: the click-clack of the heels of the shop girls marching up the street; the flushed cheeks of the uniformed high school students pouring into town for sweets, chattering away with piping Scots voices; the rain puddles reflecting the scudding clouds. Everything seemed brushed by magic. It may sound absurd, but that's the way it was.

We drove north to the Quiraing, another favorite spot. On the way you wondered if there were not other terms for the Golden Rectangle. And, of course, there are. It is sometimes called the Golden Section, the square root of 3 rectangle, the Whirling Square, and perhaps other names as well.

"What I like about it symbolically," you summed up, "is that the square of matter gives birth to all of this wonder, with the help of the arcs of the circle of spirit. The spiraling is not just an intellectual concept; it really exists spontaneously, all by itself, all over the place. Whoever discovered this must have felt as if he were looking at Sophia face to face!"

"She must have been delighted to be discovered," said I. "That's what Jung said consciousness is for."

"It makes you feel like the whole earth is a temenos, a sacred place."

We stopped at Kilt Rock, a high cliff overlooking the blue Atlantic where sun, wind, water, and rock met. There we held hands in silence and in wonder.

OF SOPHIA

Sophia is a holy Spirit.
Sophia is comforter, kind, active,
well-meaning, well-doing, all-powerful.
Sophia is a transformer
one so pure that she pervades and permeates all things.
Sophia is found by those who seek her.
Just thinking about her
brings understanding.
She will appear to you when you seek her
coming to meet you in your every thought.

—Paraphrased from *The Wisdom of Solomon*

SOPHIA SPEAKS

The Lord created me at the beginning of his works,
before all else that he made, long ago.
Alone I was fashioned
at the beginning, long before earth itself.
When there was yet no ocean I Sophia was born,
no springs brimming with water.
Before the mountains were settled in their place,
long before the hills, I Sophia was born,
when as yet he had made neither land nor lake
nor the first clod of earth.
When he prepared the heavens, I was there;
when he set a compass upon the depths.
When he set the clouds above,
when he strengthened the fountains of the deep.
Then I was as master workman at his side each day,
his darling and his delight,
playing in his presence continually,
playing on the earth when he had finished it,
while my delight was in mankind.
Hearken unto me, my children,
for blessed are they that keep my ways.
I am a tree of life to them
that find me and happy is everyone
who loves me.

—Paraphrased from *The Book of Proverbs*

XIV

Pentacles and P's and Q's

A few years ago, when we were living in Los Angeles, a friend suggested that we visit a psychic, whom she found to be remarkable. So, in the spirit of adventure, we did. We climbed the stairs to a regular office room, where a petite, dark-haired woman practiced her profession. She was, indeed, remarkable.

When I first sat down, she instructed me that I could say "yes," "no," or "please amplify." Otherwise I was not to interrupt her. Then she closed her eyes. Her first question to me was, "Skye? Is there such a place as Skye, the Isle of Skye?"

Naturally I responded with a "yes, please amplify." After all, I had once planned to retire and live there.

The woman then proceeded to describe an alleged former life of mine as a chieftain, living on Skye, in the early century when Christianity was first coming to that island. She described me as being stout, white-haired, and wearing some felt frontal piece with an emblem on it. I had gathered my people together and was holding a sword up in one hand and a ceremonial cup in the other. I was requiring the people to take a solemn oath that they would speak of our beliefs to no strangers. The time was coming when our religion would be silenced and replaced with something new, but it would never die out. Our beliefs would re-emerge in future times and be understood. They would enrich what was coming.

I confess I found this part of the reading strangely moving, especially as from my childhood up, I had always wanted to attend fancy dress parties as a Scottish chief. I first visited Skye, twenty-five years ago, and I have returned there as many times as I have returned to Iona. I have always loved it. Before meeting you, I actually traveled there one December to be sure that if I did live there, I would know what I was in for in a real sense. But then I met you, and all my plans changed. So we visit a might-have-been and enjoy it when we do.

I am relating this because if there were any truth to my past as a chieftain (and I simply enjoy the fancy without insisting upon it in any way), the place that the swearing took place would have to be the Quiraing. It is both a safe and a hidden spot. When you gaze up at it from below, it looks like a gigantic rotten tooth formed of pinnacles of black rock. It is usually lost in mist and fog and gives a first impression of being terribly spooky.

To get up there, you have to drive on a winding, one-track road, up, up, and up, devoutly praying that you will not meet an oncoming vehicle. When you do arrive, there is now a safe place to park a car, and you can walk higher and climb still higher until you turn around and behold a view like no other. Two small lochans or ponds across a drop of empty emerald air shine ghostly silver in the laps of the tumbling craggy mountains. These fall away in the distance in successive waves of dark blue-browns to greys to white light.

The majesty and the brooding power of this spot is an experience in itself. The hole of the "tooth" provides a perfect corral. There are tales of the clansmen hiding the women and cattle there during times of threat and danger. It is as dramatic a spot as one could imagine, a perfect place for oath-taking. Its grandeur puts nature in command. I have never met a local crofter or tenant farmer there; the population is extremely sparse in this northeast part of Skye called Trotternish.

This day we faced no dangers. We met only a weary, elderly man with a backpack, who was grateful for a lift halfway up the mountain. The weather was fresh and breezy, and the sky was full of billowing clouds, some still rain-swollen and not sure of what to do about the weather. We struggled up the steep mountain side and finally came to rest on a rocky ledge, since the turf was wet as a sponge. There were sheep droppings everywhere, like piles of little olives, and quite a few black-faced sheep quietly roamed about, cropping the dark, wet grass.

With a big, joint sigh, we both plopped down and stared out into limitless space, in silence and peace. Then you told me that you had spent much of the previous night thinking, if not dreaming, about pentagrams.

"Tell me what you associate with them," I suggested.

"The first thing that comes to mind is Leonardo's famous drawing of a man with arms and legs extended and his head forming the top of the star. I seem to

recall that it is symbolic of man and his mental
capacities. Is that right?"

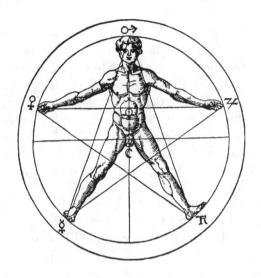

"That's right. Especially when the star is pointed
upright. When it is reversed, it has a quite sinister
meaning. It forms the head of a goat, and the Old
Goat was considered evil. This is the pentagram that
occultists associate with black magic and spells
and incantations. So, as a symbol, it offers choices.
But a pentagram—like the symbol for yin and yang,
which has a dot of black in the white and a dot of
white in the black—can contain its opposite in alter-
nating succession.

"In terms of Jungian psychology, the pentagram suggests our unconscious Shadow side. We each carry within us something we are scornful of and try to deny, so we tend to project it out onto other people. The pentagram, however, teaches us that within our upside down star another upright one can be found. Even our worst inner dragons may be roosting on pearls of wisdom, if only we have the courage to confront and befriend them. This is not easy, as all the fairy tales remind us," I added with a deep and knowing sigh.

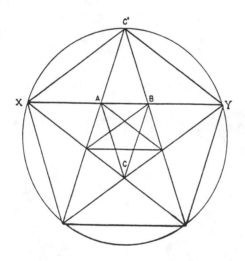

"The Greeks were more detached about the properties of the Shadow. I think the morality part came in a long time later. In Christian terms, the Greeks were quite amoral. Sex was not an issue; heroism was. I don't think of ancient Greece as a wizardy place, do you?" I asked.

"They had witches and oracles though, and pretty

spooky priestesses," you laughed. "But they were women, not wizards," you added lamely.

"Mmmmm," I murmured, not sure if you were being chauvinistic. But, quite honestly, no one would accuse you of that.

"What did the Greeks think about the pentagram?"

"Well, for them it was the shape of the number 5. And 5 is important because it is the midpoint between 1 and 10. Furthermore, it is the sum of 2 + 3, so the Greeks considered it androgynous, a union of even and odd. And since the pentagram is made up of the four lengths present in the Golden Rectangle, it was pretty special. There are so many examples of this in nature: in flowers, in starfish and sand dollars, in the proportions of the human body, even in the ratio of the segments of our fingers." Here I made a fist showing the spiral curve made by one's thumb and forefinger.

"You can fit a pentagram into a pentagon, and when you do, it makes space for more and more pentagrams," I went on.

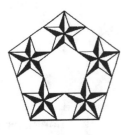 

"Also in many cultures people noticed that the pentagram is a revolving figure, so it signifies eternal action."

"How does it revolve?"

"If you touch the points, skipping one each time, you go on forever. You never come back to rest. It's sort of like cross-weaving. Perhaps for this reason, it was associated with Hermes or Mercury, or Thoth, his equivalent in Egypt. Pentacles or pentangles were symbols of commerce, and *Merc-ury* is hidden in that word."

"I suppose they are used upside down in the Black Market," you quipped, and I almost pushed you off the rock.

"What is the word for *pentagram* in German?" I asked.

You thought for a moment, and then you looked amazed. "It's called a *Drudenfuss*, a druid's foot."

"That must be because the Druids wore pentagrams on their sandals."

"How do you know all of this silly stuff?"

"I have wonderful dictionaries of symbols, and I snoop around a lot. It's fascinating, and it's fun. It's Sophia's game," I explained.

"I don't think I can ever just overlook a pentagram again," you said. "I had no idea there were that many shapes to wisdom. It's amazing."

"Can you stand more?"

"Do I have a choice?" you grinned.

"Some Christian mystics associate the pentagram with Christ as both God and man. It is the Logos aspect of reason and word. Jesus bore five wounds at the crucifixion; these are sometimes associated with the five senses that make us vulnerable to objective experience. That is a serious thought, but there is truth to it. The five also symbolize the five elements, with the fifth called the quintessence—

ether—a subtle element permeating space itself. These are the factors that could be said to wound us, because we live in their world."

"I think that's a very passive way of looking at it," you remarked. "I don't much like the idea of being programmed only to suffer in this world, though I have had my share, like anybody else."

"Well, for many centuries that has been a mindset or *Weltanschauung*. I think both Sophia and her spirit in Jung have tried to change that. We suffer because we have egos that are malfunctioning. One of the characteristics of saints, both Eastern and Western, is joy. Wisdom is joyous. Ignorance may be bliss, but it sure doesn't last! Jesus said that we had to learn to suffer and not to suffer. That's, perhaps, a way of saying that we have to be able to watch ourselves suffering with detachment, the way a mother watches her two-year old screaming its head off. She knows that this, too, will pass." Whereupon two sheep baa-ed to and fro to each other in complete agreement.

We then changed the subject. You got out your camera, while I prepared a snack of thermos tea and some bought chocolate biscuits that promised on the box that they contained "some smashing orangey bits." They sure did.

On the drive back, we shared another of Sophia's games, the joys of etymology or the study of word origins. Words are clues to the history of human thinking and evolution, and to the spreading of different people to different regions. As my friend Russell Lockhart wrote, "Words are eggs"—eggs, within eggs, within eggs.

"What is the Gaelic, do you suppose, for *five*?" you mused.

"My mother, whose grandmother was Welsh, told me that she used to count in a Welsh skipping song. It always made me laugh. It went 'An, tan, hethera, pethera, pimp'; so it was *pimp*. What's curious is that here you get the difference between Brythonic and Goidelic so clearly. The Brythonic spoken by the Welsh, Bretons, Manx, and Cornish (whose language is now extinct), uses the *p* sound, and the Goidelic spoken by the Irish and the Scots uses the *q* sound. So *pedwar*, four, and *pimp*, five, are Brythonic, and *cathair* and *coic* are Goidelic. You can see it more clearly in the French *quatre* and *cinque*. In Sanskrit, it is *panc*."

"I suppose *four* and *five* come from the Germanic *vier* and *fünf*, since *p*s and *f*s are interchangeable in those languages."

"You know how many MacDonalds and MacLeods and Mcs there are in Scotland and Ireland, and that *Mac* means 'son of.' Well, in Wales it used to be *Map* instead of *Mac*, like MapOwen. They dropped the *Ma* and the names became Bowen, Pritchard, Price (son of Rhys), and Bevan, son of Evan. Powell is the son of Hywl or Howell. There are lots of other examples.

"That reminds me of a funny story. I once traveled the British Isles with a group of American teenagers. When we finally arrived in Scotland, one disgruntled girl went off for a walk by herself and sat down on a bench beside a Scottish woman. The girl was missing American food already, so she turned reproachfully to the woman and said 'Don't you have any McDonalds over here?' To which the Scotswoman answered, wide-eyed with amazement, 'Och, dearie, but we have *thousands* of them!' "

It was late when we got back to Sligachan, but it had been a wonderful day. The stars were out, and it was hard to go inside, but we had to pack and prepare for our return to Iona the next day.

There is a postscript for this chapter. A few days after writing it, I received a letter from an old friend, who lives three hundred miles away. She is a Hungarian lady in her eighties, deeply interested in Jung. It seems she often dreams of me. The aptness of her latest dream was too good not to mention:

> Dearest Alice, it was so wonderful to hear your voice— it was like in my dream, when you walk along the seashore collecting shells—what turns into books. Then again you walk on a long street—with old stone houses—and children come out and ask you questions. Then again you are in the middle of a meadow and draw with your staff a big square, in the middle you put your staff and fresh water sprinkles from it.

So far, Woodstock, my "staff," has not taken to sprinkling, but otherwise the synchronicity is just so.

Seek him from out thyself, and learn who it is that taketh possession of everything in thee, saying: my god, my spirit, my understanding, my soul, my body; and learn whence is sorrow and joy, and love and hate, and waking though one would not, and sleeping though one would not, and getting angry though one would not, and falling in love though one would not. And if thou shouldst closely investigate these things, thou wilt find Him in thyself, The One and The Many, like to that little point, for it is in thee that He has his origin and his deliverance.

—Monoïmus

The world was the creation of the smile of Sophia.

—Valentinian Gnostics

We ought not to be weary of doing little things for the love of God, who regards not the greatness of the work, but the love with which it is performed.

—Brother Lawrence

We don't get any education in the university or church or even modern homes today which lead us inward. So a part of life remains unrevealed to us, and we only get the husk of life.

—Swami Rama

Geometry reflects nature's internal order. A simple flower like the snow iris manifests four distinct stages of development: the seed, the stem, the bud, the flower. Likewise spatial form develops in four stages: point, line, plane, and volume. The seed is the point; the plant's young shoot, stretching toward the sun, is a line. When the petals of the iris unfurl, it stabilizes in a plane. Finally the full-blown flower creates volume.

—Rachel Fletcher, geometer (1992)

XV
Sixes and Sevens

We arrived back on Iona late the following day. Autumn had brought the region a lovely new palette of orange and yellow in leaves, rich tawny brown in the bracken, interspersed with the dark green of fir trees and larches, and accented by splashes of red rowanberries. As we passed through the towering mountains on either side of Glencoe, we saw our first snow of the year dusting their tops. It was cold and bracing, cold enough for mittens.

There were few passengers on the small ferry to the island, just some returning inhabitants and young people bound afresh for their experience at the Community of the abbey. Once ashore, we walked slowly and gratefully up through the grassy greensward of the nunnery ruins, carefully closing the small iron gate behind us. We paused at Maclean's high cross, the oldest of the three great crosses on Iona, and then admired the rows of onions drying over a fence in the hotel vegetable patch. The solid grey form of the abbey loomed in the distance. It looked the stronghold that it is.

Once back in our room, we unpacked and rested before dinner. All day we had been reviewing the many connections between Jung and sacred geometry, the geometry of being. But now it was time for a good hot meal and an occasion to observe any new guests. Indeed, there was a solitary young woman at a table nearby. She wore a bright red sweater and hanging from a gold chain around her neck was a large sparkling crystal pendant. It caught the evening light and refracted it every time she bent over her plate. The woman seemed sad and lonely, while the crystal was so joyous. It was clear that she could not see the light she was radiating.

Jung had always been fascinated by the lattices of crystals. He likened the functioning of archetypes to these lattices. Because the lattice pre-exists and prefigures what the crystal is to become, the pattern is there for the crystal to follow. The same is true of archetypes in the collective psyche, where they appear as figures on the grand scale of mythology, and in the personal psyche, where they appear as structures in the unconscious. They dress themselves in dreams and in the pressures that move us though we would not be moved.

On the wall of my study I have a photograph of a painting made by Jung called "The Crystal." It was given to me by the late Dr. James Kirsch, one of Jung's oldest friends. It is a most beautiful painting of a web of white lines intersecting over an azure background. I am deeply compelled and moved every time I look at it. I have never seen it in any book of Jung's or any written about him, and I knew nothing of its history when I got it.

One day not long ago a client came to see me, a man from New York. He walked into the room and gasped. It seemed that he had spent the last few years trying to track down a copy of that very painting. He told me the following story:

He had gone to Zurich during the winter, and having been a lifelong student of Jung's works, he decided to attempt to visit Bollingen, Jung's lakeshore retreat, which he had built himself. My client had been told Bollingen would be closed to visitors, but he went anyway, just to walk around and get the feel of the place. By good fortune, he entered the stone courtyard and found the door to the house open. Jung's grandson and wife were there, and they kindly invited him in and even gave him a tour. Up the stairs in the tower, I believe, there was one special room that had been Jung's inner sanctum, which was always kept locked. The grandson, however, seeing the visitor's eagerness, unlocked the door and invited him in. The wife went to the window and opened the shutters, allowing the sunlight to fall directly upon this beautiful painting. It took the man's breath away. The room itself, he said, was monastic—plain, and sparsely furnished. The power of the painting on the wall dominated the room.

"To think that I had to travel so far and so long and then find precisely what I was seeking in a remote country house in the Berkshires," he exclaimed. "It's unbelievable. What a synchronicity!" I told

him that he had given me a precious gift, too. I had
no idea that this painting hung in Jung's inner
sanctum. It is the inspiration for the title of this
book, as it has shown me how much regard Jung
had for the web of the lattice.

Going back to the review we had been making
of the connections between Jung's concepts and
geometry, we had found the following:

—You and I had discussed Self and ego in terms
of the circle and its center, with the radius as the
"Only Way."

—We had considered extraversion as the ego's
attention focused outside the circle, and introversion
as attention directed to the contents within the circle.

—We had seen the transcendent function in terms
of the triangle balancing the opposites and lifting
them to a higher level of understanding.

—We had detected the Shadow in the inverted
pentagram and discovered its potentially positive
aspect.

Now you asked, "What about the anima and the
animus?"

We had addressed this when we talked about the
triad. Now we thought about it again and how Jung
described the relationship between a man and a
woman as fourfold: he and she, and his anima and
her animus. The minute there is a confrontation
between a man and a woman, these archetypes are
constellated: the woman becomes more logical and
rational, and the man becomes more emotional in

response. The way Jung put it, when this happens, neither the logic nor the emotions are of the highest variety. Such a situation suggests the following pattern:

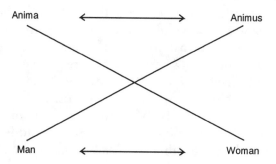

This pattern is rectangular and stressful. However, the positive function of either animus or anima within the psyche is potentially one of balance and harmony, if not of love. It is the interpenetration of two triangles in the hexagram. Moreover, as you pointed out, each triangle's angles add up to 180 degrees. Both together yield the totality of 360 degrees. We need each other for completion!

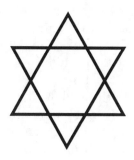

It is almost self-explanatory as a symbol of perfect union between all opposites, as well as between the masculine and the feminine. The six points within the circle form six sextiles (60 degrees), a harmonious aspect and arrangement. It is the shape of the beautiful snow crystals, the cells in the honeycomb, and of many, many flowers. Often the flowers themselves contrast the two triangles by color. Irises and some lilies and daffodils are good examples.

As we discussed this, the little bouquet of wildflowers in the vase on our table positively glowed with pleasure. Or else we did. "And to think that so many of them smell nice besides," you added.

"Consider the lilies, consider the daisies, the gentians, the roses. Having eyes, I never really saw them before in this way. It gives one so much more to consider," I mused.

"Having noses, I never smelled them," you added solemnly, and I kicked you under the table. We raised our glasses and toasted the posies.

It occurred to me that the hexagram suggests a symbol for Sophia herself. Her motto is *Ego coniungo* (I unite), and the union of two equilateral triangles is the most harmonious one imaginable. Any energies joining forces at 120 degrees join in a peaceful confluence, just as any two meeting at 90 degrees cause friction and turbulence. So the geometric symbol, and, in fact, the number 6, whose shape it is, are traditionally associated with love and harmony. (It is unfortunate that for many the association is almost exclusively the yellow Star of David that the Nazis forced the Jews to wear during the years of their persecution, though many wore it proudly. The actual color attributed by tradition to the hexagram is a clear turquoise blue, Sophia's color according to the vision of the Russian mystic Solovyov. I find it pleasing that this is also the color of the United Nations peace-keeping forces.

"Iamblichus considered 6 the perfect number because it could be divided by 1, 2, and 3. He called it the *hexad* and found it symbolic of marriage and union," I said.

"But wasn't 6 a sacred number for the Sumerians?"

"Yes, it was. All their cosmogony was based on multiples of 6, because time and circles are conveniently divided by that number. It is also the 6 directions, counting up and down, as in the 6 faces of the cube."

"What about 7?"

"7 is to 6 as 13 is to 12."

"In what way?"

"I think we have to draw it."

So after supper, we drew the following:

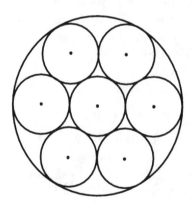

It shows clearly that six circles can be inscribed around a central one the same size. It is the picture of a week, with Sunday in the middle, just as in three dimensions twelve spheres can cluster around a central one, forming a symbol for the year with the sun at its center, or for Jesus with twelve disciples, or for Mt. Olympus with the twelve gods, or for Yahweh and the twelve tribes of Israel. Twelve is an archetypal number, a solar number, symbolic of totality. As dodecaphiles, we already had a long list of "twelves" in our workbook. (See the appendix.)

"Each number seems to have a special character, doesn't it," you remarked. "And they all get along together."

"And every single number is a fraction of the One, the Monad. So if you added everything up together, it would have to end up being One. Uni-verse. Un-ique!"

It may all seem obvious, but I am still surprised at how few people give these things even a passing thought. When they do, they are as amazed and delighted as I am. "There is no safer place for ultimate wisdom to hide than in the obvious." I quoted Mercy Muchmore, always a safe bet.

Just before falling asleep that night, you added, "I'm still glad that we are two."

"Me, too!" I replied.

The ancients considered 3, 7, and 12 to be especially important: 3 we had discussed; 7 is 3 + 4; and 12 is 3 x 4. It is easy to see how these numbers dominate Christian symbolism. The 3 is a favorite of the Celts especially (news always comes in threes), and you find it not only in the Irish love of the shamrock, but in the triplet notes that introduce so much of

Celtic music. Examples of these three numbers are everywhere. It is a challenge to make a list of them and add to it through the years.

"I keep thinking how interesting it is to look at numbers symbolically. I don't understand why it never occurred to me before," you wondered. "It's phenomenal how doing this can open doors that remained closed to our previous understanding. I can see that now. If I hear any number emphasized in a myth or a fairy tale or in ancient scriptures in the future, I will stop and ask why. They seem to have symbolic signatures as well."

"That's exactly what Jung did. He asked himself, for instance, why in fairy tales so often three sons fail and a fourth, who is a cripple or a swineheard or a foolish one, ends up the winner. He saw in that a reflection of his four functions, the inferior one leading the individual to the unconscious and towards individuation and wholeness.

intuition	thinking
sensation	feeling

"Each of us instinctively chooses to use the one of these four that comes easiest to us. This becomes the superior function, and its opposite is the inferior one, the one that we have the least confidence in. My own inferior one, as you know only too well," I said rather sheepishly, "is sensation. When we were newlyweds this soon became apparent to you."

"On the other hand," you added gallantly, "when you really apply that function, it never fails to be sensational!"

"I call it being resourceful under stress."

"Naturally, we tend to disdain our inferior function when we find it as the superior function in someone else," I commented. "Jung himself found the differences in functions a reconciling explanation for his difficulties with Freud."

This quartet of Jung's eventually became an octet when he added extraversion and introversion to each of the functions. There are several excellent books on the topic and tests, such as Meyers-Briggs and Singer's to determine one's proclivities. Knowing your typology is extremely helpful, because you become convinced that there are other legitimate ways of perceiving or judging situations, which leads to greater tolerance and understanding. Such tests are fun to take. There is no way you can fail one; everybody wins.

❖   ❖   ❖

"Why are baptismal fonts so often eight-sided octagons?" you asked.

We were making our last visit to the abbey, as the time for our departure neared. The huge stone font is the first thing one encounters as one enters the door.

"Because eight was believed to be the number of transformation and renewal. In baptism, we are supposed to become twice-born, having renounced 'the pomps and vanities of this wicked world.' "

"I know that baptism is a sacrament," you said, "an outward and visible sign of an inward and spiritual grace. But maybe it is not as simple as it seems. Maybe, in the psychological sense, it means renouncing or remaining aware of all the ego traps.

I definitely do not believe that the intrinsic nature of this world is wicked. It only seems that way if we have forgotten the Divine Guest and don't see what Sophia is trying to reveal to us. When we look with a loving eye, we will always see beauty. That way we could be baptized afresh everyday with the morning dew."

I knew what you were thinking. You were thinking of how at home during the summer we breakfast outdoors in our gazebo and count our wealth in dazzling jewels sparkling wet on the lawn from the dew which comes like a blessing on every smallest blade of grass, flower, insect, bird and beast. Since we get up so early, we often watch the sun rise and see its shafts of light turn our woods into a cathedral. The mist is mercy in action. At such times, we often quote the Sanskrit prayer:

As the sun shines upon my heart,
so may my heart shine upon others.

And we invite the Divine Guest to savor through us the hot coffee, the orange juice, and the toast and marmalade.

I honestly believe this invitation is accepted. When you make this a practice, you include the Self, and then you feel doubly blessed. Years ago, before I understood this, I always felt guilty when I was happy and fearful that I would lose everything. This is quite a common experience, almost a superstition—the gods will be jealous. This is the ego's fear. It is absolved simply by inviting the "gods" to share in being mortal. This was the teaching of the Parisian cook, Brother Lawrence, recorded in his letters,

The Practice of the Presence of God, a small treasure of a book. He is immortalized in our kitchen at home in the monkly brown trash can that came new into our family at our wedding reception. It held the ice. Actually, we have two: Brother Lawrence presides in the kitchen and Brother Juniper lives in the mudroom holding the dog food and the birdseed.

Silly as it sounds, naming common things around the house is a source of great pleasure. Jung did the same, he confessed, at Bollingen. When, after our wedding, I joined you in Los Angeles, I discovered that we had a garbage disposal machine in our kitchen sink. I had never met one before. You explained to me how it worked. "The funny thing is," you told me, "the first time I used it, I put three oranges down and they came up in the washing machine!"

"His name must be Prokofiev of 'The Love of Three Oranges.'" Thus Prokofiev joined the family, and I got a big kick out of the terrible growly-wowly noises that he made every time I shared some scraps with him. I really felt a pang at leaving him when we moved east.

At Rosecroft, we put things to freeze in "Niflheim," the Norse locale of creation, when the world was all ice. I am writing this with the help of "Leonardo," whose talents as a word processor vastly outnumber my own. He grunts a greeting, and I grunt back. It is a rich source of fun to anthropomorphize, and we find that our children and guests all take to it as well. Again, it is a way of playing Sophia's games.

I suppose this is a confession of mild insanity, but then again, perhaps it isn't. To anthropomorphize is to project as Proclus describes, but we have a defender in Paracelsus who spoke of *das Zuwerfen der Natur*—the active projection coming out of nature at us. This is a tremendous concept, because we usually perceive nature as passive and inert. Nature shouts in silence. Like Enkidu, the wild man of the *Epic of Gilgamesh*, we lost the capacity to understand its language in exchange for consciousness. When the Self in the psyche looks out through the loving eye, we will regain the capacity to see and hear nature on another level. So playing with Sophia, we meet simple objects and nature halfway, and the delight is doubled. It is a practice common to children. The trick is not to forget to do it. Then one can become more and more adept at finding things hidden within other things and acquire a certain access to secret joys.

The morning of our last day on Iona, I looked out the window as I lay lazily in bed. I noticed a single stalk of foxglove waving stiffly to and fro right past our windowsill. I was struck by its vigor and verticality. It looked like the number 1. This in turn reminded me of a most moving Sufi story told by Hazrat Inayat Khan about the power of the first letter in the Arabic alphabet—the letter *alif*, which also looks like the number 1 and, as the Arabic form of the letter *A*, begins the name of Allah.

The story, as I remembered it, goes as follows:

> There was once a great Indian sage called Bullah who as a boy went to school with other boys. The teacher began the lessons with the alphabet and the first letter *alif*. Bullah was so consumed with this letter that he could learn no other. His companions learned the whole alphabet, but Bullah could only draw *alif*. Finally, the teacher sent the boy home, deciding he was retarded. Bullah suffered so much humiliation that he eventually ran away from home and lived in the forest.
>
> There, still intoxicated with the power of *alif*, he saw the letter everywhere. He saw it rising in every blade of grass, in every tree, in every flower. He felt it in the mountains, in the flames of fire, and in the upright forms of men and women. Everything to him was *alif*. He was overwhelmed again and again by the primal power of that one letter. He decided that he must now return after many years to thank his teacher.
>
> Needless to say, the teacher did not recognize the pupil who was thanking him profusely for his great lesson. Bullah told him that now that he understood the first letter, he was ready to learn the rest. The teacher was amazed that his dunce of a pupil had remembered him, and he invited Bullah to draw the letter on the wall.
>
> Bullah went to the wall and carefully drew the letter *alif*. As the teacher looked at it, the letter miraculously divided itself into two, and the man fell to his knees before his pupil in awe. "You have taught me in this hour something I had not known from all my learning." And Bullah thereafter became a great sage and teacher himself.

I closed my eyes and felt the uprushing, the up-pushing, of life everywhere. Like fire all of life defies gravity and seems to be reaching for its origin in the sun's warmth and love. I stretched and sighed with pleasure.

"My beloved spake, and said unto me, 'Rise up, my love, my fair one, and come away!' " Quoting the Song of Solomon, you held out your hand to me. "I smell coffee and toast."

We had one more lovely day before us, the gift of Iona.

Truth is within ourselves; it takes no rise
From outward things, whate'er you may believe.
There is an inmost centre in us all,
Where truth abides in fulness; and around,
Wall upon wall, the gross flesh hems it in,
This perfect, clear perception—which is truth.
A baffling and perverting carnal mesh
Binds it, and makes all error: and to KNOW
Rather consists in opening out a way
Whence the imprisoned splendour may escape,
Than in effecting entry for a light
Supposed to be without.

—Robert Browning

The central postulate of the Way is that there is a hidden
meaning in all things. Everything has an outer as well as
an inner meaning. Every external form is complemented
by an inner reality which is its hidden eternal essence. . . .
In order to know a thing completely one must not only
seek its outward and ephemeral reality but also its essential
and inward reality—that in which the eternal beauty of
every object resides.

—Nader Ardalan & Laleh Bakhtiar

Every beloved object is the focus of a paradise.

—Novalis

The highest form of attention is spiritual attention.

—Simone Weil

XVI
The Web at Work

There are several craft shops on Iona—a fine pottery, and a gift shop filled with Celtic treasures and souvenirs, to say nothing of postcards. We usually save our shopping for the last day, so that we can gauge what we will have room for in our luggage and what we can carry.

Gift shops always smell interesting, and the Iona Craft Shop was no exception, since it featured heathery cosmetics and soaps done up daintily with purple and lavender satin ribbons. What intrigued me the most was the coming together of articles, jewelry, books, ceramics, all with designs that were filled with historical allusions: a dish towel with a replica of St. Mark from the Book of Kells; silver brooches of the most complicated interwoven Celtic knot designs that might well have come with the Celts as they wandered westward across Europe from Scythia; fisherman sweaters of heavy Aran wool, each with a different design of ladders or moss, honeycomb or bobble stitches. These designs shared with the Irish may have come from Northern Africa as far back as the fifth century, since the Celtic

241

Christians were far more in touch with the Church
there than with Rome, a cause later for contention
at the Synod of Whitby. The Coptic crosses and
Coptic designs greatly resemble the designs knitted
into these heavy white jerseys. The one you were
wearing was already ten years old, but it is eyed
suspiciously every year by customs, nevertheless.

I drifted from one crowded counter to another,
imagining the many industrious fingers at work
over the winter months, knitting, knitting, knitting
in the Fair Isles, the Orkneys, or the Outer Hebrides.
These colorful patterns all have a history as well,
and the wool is often hand-dyed and hand-spun.
There were a few scarves of lacy wool from the
Orkneys that once were so fine they could be drawn
through a wedding ring. I picked up a pullover and
held it to my face, loving the lanolin smell from
the sheep, which is left in to make it waterproof.

Probably in a backroom there were a few bolts of
Harris tweed and woven tartans, each with a name
for the sett or the clan. But on Iona one is never
assaulted with the dizzying display of Scottish
gimcracks that knock your eyes out with clashing
colors on the mainland. The colors of the Hebrides
are soft and subtle, like the people. The islanders
are still today more mystical, musical, and poetic
than the highlanders. They differ in temperament
from the grand warrior spirit touted in the Highlands.
When I went to Oban (the port from which the ferry
sailed to Mull), that time in the winter, I was amazed
to find that the people had taken the country back
for themselves. There was not a single tartan item
anywhere in sight. The shop windows in the city
featured dark wool turban hats, lingerie, and magenta

satin slippers. On Skye, I had to ask a lady for some postcards. She had them stored away in a shoebox in the back. "Aye," they say of themselves, "the Scots are canny when it comes to the tourists."

Since it was now September, things were on sale, and so we bought a few small items to bring back for family and friends. My pockets and packed shoes were already full of small stones from Iona, mute little missionaries of Sophia. I place the ones I have kept in water in a glass bowl. They are my winter flowers, glowing in the wet.

I picked up a small silver pendant. It was a trefoil, simple and feminine. It reminded me of the triple aspects of the goddess in all traditions: maiden, matron, crone. I touched each point in turn, knowing and feeling within myself all three. It is strange, but even as a little girl, the crone was waiting in me. I had the fantasy that when my hair was snow-white, the inside and the outside would match. This day it was just the opposite. The child in me wanted to skip and run and twirl and dance in the garden of the nunnery. And the woman in me wished she had met you forty years earlier and had known you when your hair was auburn and you rode tall in the cavalry. I remembered your asking me so poignantly, "What color was your hair before it turned white?"

All those powers of three presented themselves: the three Hindu gunas or energies as solid, fluid, or volatile; the three Graces; the three Fates; the three-times-threes that make nines—the months of gestation; the nine Muses and Valkyries; the enneagram.

A prism flashed a rainbow from the window. It was four-sided (3+1), a tetrahedron, reminding me of the fact that it takes four to break white light into the sevenfold spectrum of the rainbow. "Look, notice, compare, and apply," whispered Mercy Muchmore in my third ear. An associative memory flashed through my mind of a wonderful anecdote about Buckminster Fuller when he was eighty-four years old. I had read it years before. I had to wait till I got home to look it up so I would get it right. Here it is, as Jeremy Bradford tells it in the journal *ONEARTH*:

> Our first meeting over breakfast in Florence ended with Bucky drawing on a paper napkin the model of Einstein's equation $E=mc^2$. "Nobody has ever been able to do so. This is the first time we have the model. It has been there all along, if only we had been able to perceive what was under our noses," he told me with infectious excitement as he pointed to the square he had drawn with two lines radiating from one corner. He had been up until 4:30 A.M. making a large model of a dodecahedron to take to pieces to demonstrate to the congress how it breaks down into simple tetrahedrons. He described how he had been folding a piece of cardboard when . . . "there it was in my hands: the model of Einstein's mathematical description of the universe. Then I saw that I held a model which showed me the mechanics of gravity. When I calculated the measurements of the edges of this tetrahedron produced by folding the cardboard, they were not as I had predicted 1.0 to infinity but were 0.99964. This puzzled me a lot, but that night I prayed and it came through me in a moment of supreme wonder that the reason the edges were less than 1.0 was because of the loss of particles due to radiation. Indeed I had been shown

not only the model of Einstein's universal equation, but also the model of the quarks." He paused, blinking away tears of emotion and peered at me through the thick lenses of his glasses. Then he smiled and added, as if sharing a blessing, "It is so perfectly, astonishingly simple." For that instant the magic of his enthusiastic description, the confidence of his disclosure that prayer and meditation had been the doorway to his understanding and the awe with which he uttered his last remark, held me spellbound, and I also perceived the wonderfilled simplicity of that until then largely incomprehensible world of physics and its language of higher mathematics.

I couldn't help thinking again of how almost anything we attend to can radiate outward in a web of associations and connect us instantly with the past and the future, as well. An example is the precious pottery mug you bought for our kitchen. I could see it on the second shelf of the cabinet when you chose it, and, indeed, there it sits next to three others, bought one at a time. When I fill it with tea, it brings me back instantly to the shop on Iona.

Sophia would also have us know that the traditional designs of all native people—African, Indian, American, South American, aboriginal—are full of hidden wisdom. The Native American weaving in our own Southwest, for instance, contains mysteries that require the weaver to be initiated. All of these designs, without exception, can be read like a book if you have the key to their symbolism.

I suddenly realized, as you were paying the

saleslady nine pounds for our purchases, that we had
not yet talked about the enneagram, so I brought it
up as we stepped out the door into an oncoming
river of pilgrims off the ferry.

We took the low road north to avoid the crowd.
This road ends in a narrow track between the higher
ground and the wild iris and grasses that grow down
to the sea. It is a muddy and rocky track, and as we
picked our way along it, we saw two people in apparent
difficulty. When we reached them, we found an old
man whose nurse companion said was in his nineties.
They had come off the previous ferry and decided
to chance the level track instead of the uphill road
to the abbey.

The old man was almost blind, red in the face
from exertion, and sweating as his city shoes slipped
on the wet stones. I handed him Woodstock, while
his nurse explained that he was "that determined"
to come to Iona, no matter what. She shook her
head behind his back at the seeming folly of it all,
but somehow I understood this need in him. With
the help of the three of us, we got him safely up to
the church and in the side door to the cool peace
of one of the choir stalls. As we sat beside him, his
white wispy hair fell this way and that, and his
rheumy blue eyes blinked with tears of gratitude.
He tried to catch his breath and sat panting, trying
to focus on something. Then he reached out his
hand, and it met mine. He gripped it and held it
fiercely, and I could feel the trembling of his whole
body through his hand. The tears now coursed down
his cheeks freely. He had made it! Somehow we shared
a secret exultation. It was one of the most moving
encounters I have ever experienced.

"We never talked about the enneagram," I remarked later on. We had returned to a spot below the track and were sitting on the grass looking over to Mull.

"What about it?"

"Well, it's one of the most outstanding examples of connecting geometry to the psyche. But the great interest in it has come since Jung lived, and I have never found any reference to it in his work. I once attended a workshop on it at the Monastery of Poor Clares in Memphis, Tennessee, where the expert was a Sister Mary Helen. She showed us how the nine points that generate the pattern can be linked with ego postures, defenses, and growth patterns. Once you recognize your own number, it is easy to see how you could grow to the next one or regress to the previous one. You follow the lines connecting the numbers. It's amazing but it really does work."

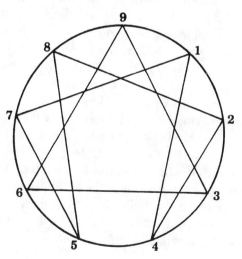

"What number am I?" you asked.

"A 7, for sure!"

"What's a 7?"

"Someone who is jovial, optimistic, positive."

"Is that bad?"

"I don't think so," I laughed.

"What are you?"

"I'm a 4, but I hope I'm improving."

"What's a 4?"

"I remember Sister Mary Helen said it was like a seagull with an arrow through its breast but it keeps flying. It fit at the time, but then I hadn't met you! I think that until I met you, I lived all of my life in a minor key."

"It sounds a bit complicated," you commented, looking out to sea, "like a geometric circuit."

"It's hard to do it justice in a few words," I responded. "The humorous way the nuns used it on each other at the monastery was wonderful. Instead of getting annoyed with one another, they readily acknowledged that someone had called their number. If one of them was martyring herself in the service of the others, you would hear 'Oh, Sister Mary Joseph, stop being a 2!' It was the quickest way imaginable to help a person to become aware of their ego playing a habitual game. And each knew exactly what the next step for growth had to be. I was profoundly impressed. I think everybody would benefit by knowing about it. I am positive Jung would have been fascinated with it and would have paid it serious attention. In some ways it is the ultimate application of geometry to the psyche. It lives because it moves. It shows how predictably we can backslide (following the line) and in what specific direction the next step lies. We were not told our number, but the minute you read the description of its characteristics you could identify yourself. It was embarrassingly accurate and hilarious at the same time."

"Who discovered it?" you asked.

"The enneagram's origin is usually attributed to Gurdjieff, and its fascinating applications to the way things work are well described by John Bennett, a student of Gurdjieff's, but I believe the psychological applications were the discovery of a Peruvian, Oscar Ichazo. Today there are lots of books available about the enneagram. We have several at home."

"It sounds fascinating," you said.

"It really is, but it is a vast subject, and it would take another book to do it justice. On the other hand, not to mention it would be a grave omission."

You stretched your legs and smiled, "How many wonders there are in this world. I hope there is reincarnation, because I really want to come back and learn some more." Then we looked at each other, and you spoke my thought. "Only next time, let's find each other sooner!"

After tea, we took another stroll and then returned to the abbey for a last visit, since we would be leaving at dawn the next day. Once again, we stood in the abbey thinking of home, just as so often we have stood in our home thinking of Iona.

Together we sat in the choir stall and prayed. Then we walked about and found a corner with cushions set round on the floor—a place where the young people of the Community had placed a list of names and causes to be prayed for. We stood before the altar. We waved to the new young warden, Philip Newell, who came out of the sacristy dressed in blue jeans and a sweatshirt—no wonder the young members loved him—and he waved back. We walked out into the cloister and circumambulated its square, admiring the old and new columns sculpted with flowers and birds. We heard the African music swelling out from a tape recorder of the abbey bookshop. We drifted into the windowless, well-lit cave-like shop, and bought more cards to keep for ourselves. Then we slowly retraced our steps into the abbey and up the aisle over the ancient heavy stones, looking for the small crosses carved into one or two of them. To walk the way of the cross now had meaning enfolded within meaning. The "Only Way" I now understood to be within me, and the cross I bear must be my own.

For me the symbol of the cross—and I do not mean to shock or diminish the Christian viewpoint—is truly universal, as are all the other geometric symbols. The Divine Guest, which for Christians is the Christ Within, is surely a light that shines in all humankind. The wisdom of Sophia is there to guide us, whatever our religion. Jung has made possible a better understanding, psychologically speaking, of what that "Only Way" consists of for each human soul. The true Teachers, known and unknown, have dropped hints in shouts and whispers and have strewn clues like seeds all about. They cannot do more than that. It is we who have to pick them up in our hearts, our homes, our gardens, our streets, and in the commonplace of our daily lives. Only thus can they bloom for us. We have to make them our own.

Sophia's secret of secrets is that all of this can make life de-light-full.

With grateful hearts, we walked out of the abbey

into the sunlight. There stood St. Martin's Cross, the cross that had started my quest for Iona in the first place, as I have recounted in *The Dove in the Stone*. Its shadow fell clearly upon the ground, proving the light. We laid our hands upon it and vowed to return, if possible, yet again. Then we turned, and holding hands walked sunwards into the future, knowing full well—thanks to Jung, Sophia, and love itself—the paradox that inward is the "Only Way" home.

The Web in the Sea

The sea is so calm that it is like silver slated all about.
Far, far off, other dark isles lie dreaming,
Floating, each on a strip of light.
Nothing moves, nothing sounds.
It seems the world sleeps in the arms of Sophia.
We sit in the cool silence, silent ourselves
Watching the stars prick out of a heaven
That is a mirror of the sea.
Such peaceful detachment
Of distant fire, earth, water, air—
They know how to be.
I let my thoughts slip away.
And for a moment, sitting beside you
I, too, remember how it is to be.

A vision comes:
Sophia is weaving a web in the sea of life.
It connects everything and everyone.
It threads from point to point of every sphere
Of every atom of every being.
The web is of beauty.
The web is of the shapes of light.
It drops to the depths into darkness.
It is hooked onto the stars. Its loom is creation.
It shimmers, it waves slowly, clearly, through time.

It is vast, it is minikin wee.
It is the weft in which we float.
It is holding, feeding us all unknowing in our blindness
Until we are ready to see.
Until we are ready to be comforted and to comfort.

I want to touch the web now that I have seen it.
I want to sing of it if I can.
I pray this prayer on Iona.
The answer comes:
Touch. Touch love.
I reach out in silence for the deep beatitude of your hand.
In touching you, or you, I touch all that you have touched
And been touched by,
Back and back and back to the beginning of beginnings.

This I now know is a truth for all:
To reach in love, to touch in kindness, is to touch
The web in the sea of Sophia—
The beauteous web she is weaving with joy and of wisdom,
The one she is weaving for God.

                                        A.O.

Where is the Life we have lost in living?
Where is the wisdom we have lost in knowledge?
Where is the knowledge we have lost in information?
The cycles of heaven in twenty centuries
Bring us farther from God and nearer to the Dust.
                                                —T.S. Eliot

As above, so below.
                    —The Emerald Tablet of Hermes Trismegistus

A line reveals a million things.
                                                —Novalis

Appendix
Sophia's Mondayschool

Materials:

> a looseleaf binder
> index tabs
> blank paper
> lined paper
> graph paper
> a compass
> a straight edge
> a protractor
> a right angle
> two sharp eyes

Procedure:

a) make separate entries for:
the geometric figures (see suggested list below)
the five solids
1,2,3,4,5,6,7,8,9,10,11,12,13 . . . and on and on
(some bigger numbers have special properties;
   collect them!)

Resources:

>nature and your immediate environment
>dictionaries of symbols (see bibliography)
>the Holy Bible (with concordance)
>sacred scriptures of any religion
>books of mythology and fairy tales
>dictionary of word origins

b) make categories for symbolic associations:

>hidden process
>nature
>mythology & folklore
>religions: Christianity, Judaism, Islam, Hinduism,
>   Buddhism, and Ancient and Native Spirituality
>philosophy
>psychological archetypes
>etymology
>literary allusions and quotations
>art and architecture
>dreams
>personal memories and insights

This should not be a task, but a joy. Do your own thing!

Sophia's *Mondayschool* suggests that we take the geometric progressions that we studied and begin to look for them in nature, in the psyche, and in our daily lives, thereby learning to think symbolically and to weave the web of interconnecting processes that catch those little silver fish of insight.

The following pages contain a few seed words that were helpful to me. As more ideas come to the reader they can be jotted down in this book. Keeping a looseleaf book tabulated to shapes and numbers can be a lifelong source of enjoyment. It is something, I understand, that Jung practiced with alchemical terms.

One day when I was doing my own research and had about twenty books stacked around me, I opened one of Jung's volumes and read the remark made by an alchemist: "One book opens another." And so it does.

The purpose of these exercises is to bring forth something everyone already has an innate gift for— thinking symbolically and so leading more joyfully what Jung called "the symbolic life." This entails another way of looking, seeing, applying, and re-connecting what we have noticed to a spiritual insight that is personally meaningful. By doing so, we put our hand in the loving one of Sophia, our inner guide to the source of wisdom and joy, the Divine Guest or Self within us, that inner light that is one with the Source of life and love.

Nature is our *vademecum*, our instruction book; its leaves speak volumes in silence.

The motto of the spiritual alchemist was:

Ora et labora. Lege, lege, lege et relege, et invenies.

(Pray and work. Read, read, read and reread, and discover.) I do not believe that this refers to actual books, since the greatest secrets could never be put into words.

I find it interesting that we can today visit either an oratory *or* a laboratory. For the spiritual alchemist and the practical mystic, these are one and the same, and we carry them in our soul.

SEED WORDS

nothing	all	blank	Brahman	being
immaculate		virgin	eternal	space
unconscious	empty	the Void	potential . . .

THE POINT

beginning	creation	spot	mote	I am
conception	becoming	focus	center	*bindu*
Brahma	no dimension	*yod*	iota . . .	

— — — — — — — — — — — — — — — —

●

THE CIRCLE

ouroboros   spirit unmanifest   boundary   limitless
totality   zero   egg   ring   girdle of Venus   Wagner
Tolkien   totality   psyche   cycle   wheel   watch
zodiac   encompassing   womb . . .

— — — — — — — — — — — — — — — — — —

CIRCLE AND CENTERPOINT

sun   gold   fertile egg   spirit manifest   individual
Christ within   Divine Guest Self   atman   eye   hub
egg & sperm   midpoint   centerpoint   unity   nucleus
cell   yolk . . .

— — — — — — — — — — — — — — — — —

CIRCLE WITH RADIUS

the "Only Way" self-ego axis clock hand way in
way out first line first dimension ego questing in
circles meditation concentration . . .

———————————————————————

CIRCLE WITH DIAMETER

duality Genesis above/below hemispheres
as above, so below . . .

THE LINE
Introduces duality.

The vertical line:

| masculine | yang | above/below | alif | plumb line |

masculine   yang   above/below   alif   plumb line
pendulum   standing stones   church steeples   tree trunks
world axis   May pole   flowering staff of Joseph of
Arimethaea   phallus   stem of Jesse   Jacob's ladder
spine   pole   rain   sun's rays   Jack and the Beanstalk
. . . (The list is almost endless, with the process implying the connection between heaven and earth, God and humanity, higher with lower and lower with higher.)

THE LINE
Introduces duality.

The horizontal line:

feminine	yin	receptive	earth	furrow	road
minus	horizon	bottom line		property lines . . .	

— — — — — — — — — — — — — — — — —

———————

FUTHER FIGURES TO
CONSTRUCT AND CONTEMPLATE

THE FIVE SOLIDS AND
HOW TO CONSTRUCT THEM

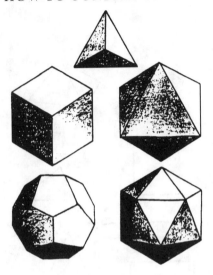

THE FIVE POLYHEDRA

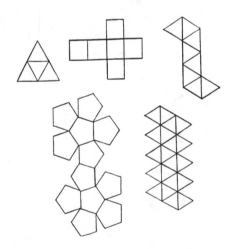

HOW TO CONSTRUCT THE FIVE SOLIDS

AN ELEGANT TRIANGULAR
PROOF OF THE GOLDEN SECTION

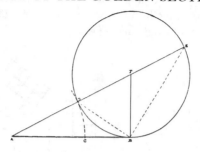

FINDING THE GREAT PYRAMID

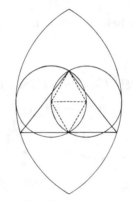

THE BEAUTY OF A PROGRESSION

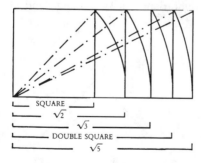

THE PYTHAGOREAN THEOREM

This is the famous and familiar theorem of Pythagoras. It states that the square of the hypotenuse equals the sum of the square of the two sides of a right angled triangle.

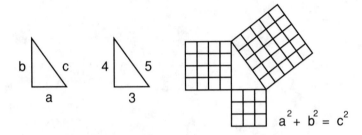

This theorem lends itself to a host of philosophical conclusions. Meditate on it.

MAKING A DRUIDS' CORD

Take a piece of string and tie twelve equally spaced knots in it.

This will give thirteen spaces. This device was used by the Egyptians for designing construction since it can form a Pythagorean right triangle, a 4,4,5 triangle and a twelve-spoked wheel.

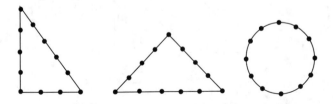

NUMBER WORD ROOTS IN GREEK AND LATIN

	Greek	Latin
1	*monas* as in monad	*monas* or *unus*
2	*dyas* as in dyad	*duo* - or *bi* -
3	*trias* as in triad	*tri* -
4	*tetras* as in tetrad	*quatr* - or *quart* -
5	*pentas* as in pentad	*quint* -
6	*hexas* as in hexad	*sex* -
7	*heptas* as in heptad	*sept* -
8	*octas* as in octad	*octo* -
9	*enneas* as in ennead	*nona* -
10	*deka* as in decad	*deci* -

❖   ❖   ❖

Suffixes:

- *gon*, side as in *pentagon* = five-sided

- *gram*, something drawn or written as in *diagram, enneagram*

- *hedra*, surface as in *tetrahedron*, a solid with four faces.

Thus a "monk" is one who lives alone and a "dodecahedron" is a twelve-surfaced solid, a "decade" is a period of ten years and a "nonagenarian" is a ninety-year old. Almost all geometrical terms come to us from the Greeks.

A COLLECTION OF TWELVES

The number 12 is associated with the sun and solar heroes, with completion and totality. To the ancients it was the multiple of the three qualities and the four quantities or elements. Whenever we encounter it, it has archetypal significance. Be a 12-watcher and add to this collection:

12 disciples/apostles

12 acupuncture meridians in the body

12 pairs of cranial nerves (24)

12 x 2 time meridians on a globe

12 tissue salts

12 hours on a watch (24 hours in a day)

12 months in a year

12 Signs of the Zodiac

12 inches to a foot

12 people on a jury

12 Constellations

12 sons of Jacob

12 running springs in Helim

12 rivers flowing from the spring Hvergelmir (Norse)

12 loaves in the Sanctuary

12 stones on Hebrew breastplate (Old Testament)

12 stones on Hebrew altar

12 Tablets of Roman law

12 Labors of Hercules

12 Olympian gods

12 dii maiores (Roman)

12 Buddhic nidanas:

12 states of emergence

12 saviors (Pistis Sophia)

12 Knights of King Arthur

12 deities on Ra's solar boat (Egypt)

12 gates of the Ming-t'ang (China)

12 fruits on the Tree of Life

12 dynamic aspect of 4x3 (female & male) for Dogons and Bambaras of Mali (Africa)

12 total of sides on two dice

12 Merry Men about Oak King

12 oxen bearing brzen sea
   at Solomon's Temple
12 stars in crown of
   Woman clothed
   with the Sun
   (New Testament)
12 foundations of
   Jerusalem
12 aeons
12 Labors of Gilgamesh
12 Meistersingers
12 Days of Christmas
12 notes to a piano scale
   (7 + 5)

12 Sacred Chinese
   Ornaments
12 Norse Gods
12 Gates to Babylon
12 episodes of Moses' life
12 exploits of Odysseus
12 Paladins of
   Charlemagne
12 in circular council of
   Dalai Lama

From the example of the "Twelves," we can see the power of an archetypal number in all cultures. Make a collection of other especially significant numbers:

> Threes (trios and trinities)
> Fours
> Fives
> Sevens (which lead to octaves [8]) as in colors, music, etc.)
> Nines
> Tens
> Thirteens
> Twenty-fours
> Forties (many in the Bible)
> Sixties
> One hundred forty-fours

As your collection grows, you will be surprised to see Sophia's web extending and resonating when various numbers are called up. For me, numbers have almost acquired personalities and characteristic behaviors. I greatly envy those theoretical physicists who are able to combine letters and numbers in an algebraic dance of supreme elegance. Alas, for me, this is a door I can only open, but, oh, how I love the sound of the music that I hear!

EGYPTIAN	PHOENICIAN	HEBREW LETTER	HEBREW SOUND	HEBREW NUMBER VALUE	HEBREW NUMBER NAME	GREEK LETTER	GREEK SOUND	GREEK NUMBER VALUE	GREEK NUMBER NAME	ROMAN	RUNES LETTER	RUNES NUMBER VALUE
𐃐	𐤀	א	'	1	alef	Αα	a	1	álpha	A	ᚠ	4
⬚	𐤁	ב	b	2	bath	Ββ	b	2	bêtha	B	ᛒ	18
	𐤂	ג	g	3	gimel	Γγ	g	3	gámma	C	–	–
⬚	𐤃	ד	d	4	daleth	Δδ	d	4	délta	D	ᛗ	24
Ψ	𐤄	ה	h	5	he	Εε	e	5	è·psilón	E	M,1	19,13
	𐤅	ו	w	6	vav	Ϝς	–	6	vaû	F	ᚡ	1
	𐤆	ז	z	7	zain	Ζζ	z	7	zêta	(G)	ᛜ	7
	𐤇	ח	h	8	heth	Ηη	ä	8	êta	H	ᚺ	9
	𐤈	ט	t	9	teth	Θϑ	th	9	thêta		ᚦ	3
⬚	𐤉	י	j	10	iod	Ιι	i	10	jôta	I	ᛁ,ᛊ	11,12
⬚	𐤊	כ	k	20	kaf	Κκ	k	20	káppa	K	ᚲ	6
	𐤋	ל	l	30	lamed	Λλ	l	30	lámbda	L	ᚱ	21
∿	𐤌	מ	m	40	mem	Μμ	m	40	mu	M	ᛗ	20
⬚	𐤍	נ	n	50	nun	Νν	n	50	nu	N	ᛏ	10
	𐤎	ס	s	60	samek	Ξξ	x	60	xî	–	–	–
⬚	𐤏	ע	'	70	ayin	Οο	o	70	o·micron	O	ᛟ	23
⬚	𐤐	פ	p	80	pe	Ππ	p	80	pî	P	ᛈ	14
	𐤑	צ	s	90	sade	–	–	–		–	–	–
⬚	𐤒	ק	q	100	gof	Ϙϙ	–	90	kóppa	Q	–	–
	𐤓	ר	r	200	resh	Ρρ	r	100	rhô	R	ᚱ	5
	𐤔	ש	š	300	shin	Σσ	s	200	sîgma	S	ᛋ	16
	𐤕	ת	t	400	tau	Ττ	t	300	taû	T	ᛏ	17
		ך	-k	(500)	(kaf)	Υυ	ü	400	y-psilon	V	u: ᚢ	2
		ם	-m	(600)	(mem)	Φφ	ph	500	phî	1000	w: ᚹ	8
		ן	-n	(700)	(nun)	Χχ	ch	600	chî	X	ng: ᛜ	22
		ף	-f	(800)	(fe)	ψ	ps	700	psî		-z: ᛇ	15
		ץ	-s	(900)	(sade)	Ωω	ō	800	o-méga			
						Ϡ	–	900	sampi			

Pythagoras

Pythagoras, of old
heard in his waking dream
the ancillary prographs of the Golden Word.
The petty petitions of the worm-eaters
as yet deferred
were as the dust unformed on my piano
wrapped in its plastic sheet
lest the music escape
and make this heart more wretched
to lose its unsung beat.
Space to him was iridescence
a scale of ordered rhapsodies
spiraling with half-furled wings
in the chromathematics
Eternal Being sings
with such grave and sweet restraint.
When he had reached the tower
of his reasoning
he found the steps back down
were black and white
triangles and ringed with fright.
What was the Greek for do, re, mi?

He must have cleaned his
trembling fingernails
to remind himself that he was mortal.

Pythagoras, of old
saw in his waking dream
the universe—a cosmic harp
with stars for streaming notes
and space for non-existent things;
the precessions of the equinox
the cadence of planets holding hands
in their stately dance of epoch
which demands
converging rays of every circle
sun-centered in wonder—

His thought yet thunders down the centuries
as some wild exultant Pegasus
scattering bright hoofprints
in our wincing minds.
Let me tell you that
his eyes in death became light mirrors of fire
and in his visions and his desire
he was blinded and could not speak.
We yet see ourselves reflected
in the square of his hypotenuse
singing mutely
do, re, mi—
Though not, of course, in Greek.

A.O.

Bibliography

Adler, Irving. 1958. *Mathematics: the study of numbers, symbols and space.* New York: Golden Press.

Alcott, A. Bronson. 1991. *How like an angel came I down: conversations with children on the gospels.* Ed. and commentary by Alice O. Howell. Hudson, NY: Lindisfarne Press.

Allendy, Dr. R. 1921. *Le symbolisme des nombres.* Paris: Bibliotheque Chacornac.

❖ Ardalan, Nader & Laleh Bakhtiar. 1979. *The sense of unity: Sufi symbolism in Persian architecture.* Chicago: University of Chicago Press.

Bakhtiar, Laleh. 1976. *Sufi: Expressions of the mystic quest.* New York: Avon Books.

Bauer, Wolfgang. 1983. *Lexikon der symbole.* Wiesbaden: Fourier Verlag.

❖ Blair, Lawrence. 1976. *Rhythms of vision.* New York: Schocken Books.

Bradford, Jeremy. 1978. Introduction to "Ever re-thinking the Lord's Prayer," by Buckminster Fuller. *Onearth* 6.

❖ Bragdon, Claude. 1922. *The beautiful necessity.* New York: Alfred A. Knopf.

Browning, Robert. 1898. *Pauline—Paracelsus.* New York: Thomas Y. Crowell & Company.

Case, Paul Foster. 1947. *The Tarot.* New York: Macoy Publishing Company.

Chevalier, Jean and Alain Gheerbrant. 1973. *Dictionnaire des symboles.* Paris: Ed. Seghers et Ed. Jupiter.

❖ These titles are especially recommended for an easy introduction to both Sophia and sacred geometry.

❖ Cirlot, J. E. 1962. A *Dictionary of symbols*. Jack Sage, tr. New York: Philosophical Library.

Coleman, Samuel. 1971. *Nature's harmonic unity*. New York: Benjamin Bloom.

Cooper, J. C. 1978. *An illustrated encyclopedia of traditional symbols*. London: Thames and Hudson, Ltd.

❖ De Vries, Ad. 1981. *Dictionary of symbols and imagery*. Amsterdam: North-Holland Publishing Co.

Edinger, Edward F. 1972. *Ego and archetype*. New York: G. P. Putnam's Sons for the C. G. Jung Society.

Emerson, Ralph Waldo. 1926. *Essays*. New York: Thomas Y. Crowell Company.

Emre, Yunus. Kabir Helminski and Refik Algan, trs. 1989. *The drop that became the sea*. Putney, Vermont: Threshold Books.

Euclid. Sir Thomas Heath, tr. *The thirteen books of Euclid's elements*. London: Encyclopaedia Britannica, Inc.

Gardner, Edward L. 1987. *The play of consciousness in the web of the universe*. Wheaton, IL: The Theosophical Publishing House.

Ghyka, Matila. 1971. *Philosophie et mystique du nombre*. Paris: Payot.

——. *The geometry of art and life*. New York: Dover Publications, Inc.

Godwin, Joscelyn. 1987. *Harmonies of heaven and earth*. London: Thames and Hudson, Ltd.

——. 1979. *Robert Fludd*. Boulder, CO: Shambhala.

Guthrie, Kenneth Sylvan. 1987. *The Pythagorean sourcebook and library*. Grand Rapids, MI: Phanes Press.

Guenon, Rene. 1953. *The reign of quantity and the signs of the times*. Lord Northbourne, tr. Baltimore: Penguin Books, Inc.

Howell, Alice O. 1987. *Jungian symbolism in astrology*. Wheaton, IL: The Theosophical Press/Quest Books.

❖ ——. 1989. *The dove in the stone*. Wheaton, IL: The Theosophical Press/Quest Books.

——. 1990. *Jungian synchronicity in astrological signs*

and ages. Wheaton, IL: The Theosophical Press/ Quest Books.

I Ching—book of changes. Vol. I. 1955. Richard Wilhelm/ Cary F. Baynes, trs. Bollingen Series XIX. New York: Pantheon Books.

Jacobs, Harold R. 1970. *Mathematics, a human endeavor.* San Francisco: W. H. Freeman and Company.

Jenny, Hans. 1974. *Cymatics, Vol. II.* Basel: Basilius Presse A. G.

❖ Jobes, Gertrude. 1962. *Dictionary of mythology, folklore and symbols (3 vols.).* New York: The Scarecrow Press.

Karagulla, Shafica & Dora van Gelder Kunz. *The chakras and human energy fields.* Wheaton, IL: Theosophical Publishing House/Quest Books.

Khan, Hazrat Inayat. 1980. *Tales told by Hazrat Inayat Khan.* New Lebanon, N.Y.: Sufi Order Publications.

Jung, C. G. 1957-1979. *The collected works.* R. F. C. Hull, tr. Bollingen Series, 20 vols. Princeton: Princeton University Press.

Khanna, Madu. 1979. *Yantra.* London: Thames and Hudson, Ltd.

Lao Tzu. 1944. *The way of life.* Witter Bynner, tr. New York: Capricorn Books.

❖ Lawlor, Robert. 1982. *Sacred Geometry.* New York: The Crossroad Publishing Co.

Lawrence, D. H. 1971. *The complete poems of D. H. Lawrence.* Vivian de Sola Pinto and Warren Roberts, eds. New York: The Viking Press.

Lehner, Ernst. 1950. *Symbols, signs, and signets.* New York: Dover Publications.

Marinus of Samaria. 1986. *The life of Proclus.* Kenneth S. Guthrie, tr. Grand Rapids, MI: Phanes Press.

❖ Matthews, Caitlin. 1991. *Sophia, goddess of wisdom.* Bath, Avon: Bath Press.

McLean, Adam. 1989. *The alchemical mandala.* Grand Rapids, MI: Phanes Press.

Menninger, Karl. 1970. *Number words and number symbols.* Paul Broneer, tr. Cambridge, MA: The M.I.T. Press.

Morrow, Glenn R. 1970. *Proclus, a commentary on the first book of Euclid's elements*. Princeton, NJ: Princeton University Press.

Neumann, Erich. 1963. *The great mother*. Princeton, NJ: Princeton University Press.

The new analytical Bible. 1964. Chicago: John A. Dickson Publishing Company.

Nicomachus of Gerasa. 1960. *Introduction to arithmetic*. Martin Luther D'ooge, tr. Annapolis, MD: St. John's College Press.

Novalis. 1989. *Pollen and fragments*. Arthur Versluis, tr. Grand Rapids, MI: Phanes Press.

Ouspensky, P. D. 1923. *Tertium organum*. London: Kegan Paul, Trench Trubner & Co., Ltd.

❖ Pennick, Nigel. 1980. *Sacred geometry*. Wellingborough, Northamptonshire: Turnstone Press, Ltd.

Perkins, James S. 1986. *A geometry of space consciousness*. Wheaton, IL: The Theosophical Publishing House.

Plato. [undated]. *The works of Plato*. New York: Tudor Publishing House.

———. 1959. *Timaeus*. Francis M. Cornford, tr. New York: Bobbs-Merrill Co., Inc.

Plummer, L. Gordon. *The mathematics of the cosmic mind*. Wheaton, IL: The Theosophical Publishing House.

Proclus. 1963. *The elements of theology*. Oxford: Clarendon Press.

Purce, Jill. 1974. *The mystic spiral*. London: Thames and Hudson.

The Oxford book of English verse. 1969. Ed, Sir Arthur Quiller-Couch. Oxford: Clarendon Press.

Raleigh, A. S. 1932. *Occult geometry*. Chicago: The Hermetic Publishing Company.

Rao, S. K. Ramachandra. 1979. *Tantra mantra yantra*. New Delhi: Arnold Heinemann Publishers.

Rice, Edward. 1980. *Eastern definitions*. Garden City, N.Y.: Doubleday and Company, Inc.

Runion, Garth E. 1972. *The golden section and related curiosa*. Glenview, IL: Scott, Foresman & Co.

Sambursky, S. 1960. *The physical world of the Greeks.* London: Routledge and Kegan Paul.

Schwaller de Lubicz, R. A. 1986. *A study of numbers.* Rochester, VT: Inner Traditions International, Ltd.

Schwenk, Theodor. 1965. *Sensitive chaos.* Olive Whicher, Johanna Wrigley, trs. London: Rudolf Steiner Press.

Singer, June. 1990. *Seeing through the visible world.* San Francisco: Harper & Row Publishers.

❖ Skeat, Rev. Walter W. 1882. *An etymological dictionary of the English language.* Oxford: Clarendon Press.

Stanley, Thomas. 1970. *Pythagoras.* Los Angeles: The Philosophical Research Society, Inc.

Strong, James. 1890. *The exhaustive concordance of the Bible.* New York: Eaton & Mains.

Sutherland, Elizabeth. 1985. *Ravens and black rain.* London: Constable.

❖ Terrenus, Aurora. 1988. *Sophia of the Bible: the spirit of wisdom.* Santa Cruz, CA: Celestial Communications, The Publishing House of the Holy Order of Wisdom.

Theon of Smyrna. 1979. *Mathematics useful for understanding Plato.* San Diego: Wizards Bookshelf.

Thompson, William Irwin. 1978. "Onearth 6 Journal: Shaping Wisdom." Findhorn, Scotland: Findhorn Publications.

Von Franz, Marie-Louise. 1974. *Number and time.* Andrea Dykes, tr. Evanston: Northwestern University Press.

Waite, Arthur Edward. [undated]. *A new encyclopedia of Freemasonry.* New York: Weathervane Books.

Walker, Barbara G. 1988. *The woman's dictionary of symbols and sacred objects.* San Francisco: Harper Collins Publishers.

Waterfield, Robin. 1988. *The theology of arithmetic.* Grand Rapids, MI: Phanes Press.

Weil, Simone. 1956. *The notebooks of Simone Weil.* 2 vols. Arthur Wills, tr. London: Routledge & Kegan Paul.

Whitmont, Edward C. 1984. *The return of the goddess.* New York: Crossroads.

Wood, Ernest. 1987. *Concentration: an approach to meditation.* Wheaton, IL: The Theosophical Publishing House.

Ora et labora. Lege, lege, lege, relege et invenies.